soups

soups

by the editors at
america's test kitchen

Library of Congress
Cataloging-in-Publication Data

Names: America's Test Kitchen (Firm)
Title: All time best soups /
  by the editors at America's Test Kitchen.
Description: Brookline, MA :
  America's Test Kitchen, [2016] |
  Includes index.
Identifiers: LCCN 2016018807 |
  ISBN 9781940352800
Subjects: LCSH: Soups. |
  LCGFT: Cookbooks.
Classification: LCC TX757 .A4384 2016 |
  DDC 641.81/3--dc23
LC record available at
  https://lccn.loc.gov/2016018807

AMERICA'S TEST KITCHEN

17 Station Street, Brookline, MA 02445

Manufactured in the United States of
America

10 9 8 7 6 5 4 3 2

Distributed by Penguin Random House
Publisher Services

Tel: 800.733.3000

Chief Creative Officer: Jack Bishop
Editorial Director, Books: Elizabeth Carduff
Executive Editor: Julia Collin Davison
Executive Editor: Adam Kowit
Senior Editor: Debra Hudak
Editorial Assistant: Alyssa Langer
Art Director: Carole Goodman
Associate Art Directors: Allison Boales and Jen Kanavos Hoffman
Production Designer: Reinaldo Cruz
Graphic Designers: Aleko Giatrakis and Sarah Horwitch Dailey
Photography Director: Julie Bozzo Cote
Assistant Photography Producer: Mary Ball
Senior Staff Photographer: Daniel J. van Ackere
Staff Photographer: Steve Klise
Photography: Keller + Keller and Carl Tremblay
Food Styling: Catrine Kelty, Marie Piraino, and Sally Staub
Photoshoot Kitchen Team:
    Senior Editor: Chris O'Connor
    Associate Editor: Daniel Cellucci
    Test Cook: Matthew Fairman
    Assistant Test Cook: Allison Berkey
Production Director: Guy Rochford
Senior Production Manager: Jessica Lindheimer Quirk
Production Manager: Christine Walsh
Imaging Manager: Lauren Robbins
Production and Imaging Specialists: Heather Dube, Sean MacDonald, Dennis Noble, and Jessica Voas
Copy Editor: Cheryl Redmond
Proofreader: Pat Jalbert-Levine
Indexer: Elizabeth Parson

Pictured on front cover: Sicilian Chickpea and Escarole Soup (page 153)
Pictured on back cover (clockwise from lower left): Quick Beef and Barley Soup (page 18), Vegetable Shabu-Shabu wth Sesame Sauce (page 105), Manhattan Clam Chowder (page 77), Mexican Beef and Vegetable Soup (page 60)

contents

viii welcome to america's test kitchen

ix introduction

x soup basics

12 weeknight workhorses

36 soups from around the world

70 chowders

86 modern vegetable soups

112 elegant purees

138 rustic bean soups

164 stocks and broths

176 conversions and equivalents

177 index

welcome to america's test kitchen

THIS BOOK HAS BEEN TESTED, WRITTEN, AND EDITED BY THE folks at America's Test Kitchen, a very real 2,500-square-foot kitchen located just outside of Boston. It is the home of *Cook's Illustrated* magazine and *Cook's Country* magazine and is the Monday-through-Friday destination for more than 60 test cooks, editors, and cookware specialists. Our mission is to test recipes over and over again until we understand how and why they work and until we arrive at the "best" version.

We start the process of testing a recipe with a complete lack of preconceptions, which means that we accept no claim, no technique, and no recipe at face value. We simply assemble as many variations as possible, test a half-dozen of the most promising, and taste the results blind. We then construct our own recipe and continue to test it, varying ingredients, techniques, and cooking times until we reach a consensus. As we like to say in the test kitchen, "We make the mistakes so you don't have to." The result, we hope, is the best version of a particular recipe, but we realize that only you can be the final judge of our success (or failure). We use the same rigorous approach when we test equipment and taste ingredients.

All of this would not be possible without a belief that good cooking, much like good music, is based on a foundation of objective technique. Some people like spicy foods and others don't, but there is a right way to sauté, there is a best way to cook a pot roast, and there are measurable scientific principles involved in producing perfectly beaten, stable egg whites. Our ultimate goal is to investigate the fundamental principles of cooking to give you the techniques, tools, and ingredients you need to become a better cook. It is as simple as that.

To see what goes on behind the scenes at America's Test Kitchen, check out our social media channels for kitchen snapshots, exclusive content, video tips, and much more. You can watch us work (in our actual test kitchen) by tuning in to *America's Test Kitchen* or *Cook's Country from America's Test Kitchen* on public television or on our websites. Listen in to *America's Test Kitchen Radio* (ATKradio.com) on public radio to hear insights that illuminate the truth about real home cooking. Want to hone your cooking skills or finally learn how to bake—with an America's Test Kitchen test cook? Enroll in one of our online cooking classes. If the big questions about the hows and whys of food science are your passion, join our Cook's Science experts for a deep dive. However you choose to visit us, we welcome you into our kitchen, where you can stand by our side as we test our way to the best recipes in America.

introduction

SOUP IS A FOOD WITH A PAST. ONE THAT CONJURES UP ALL KINDS of pleasant food memories: Grandma's matzo ball soup, Dad's corn chowder, tomato soup from that famous red and white can, or umpteen packages of ramen consumed in college. There is no question that few dishes are as satisfying as a bowl of soup, the original one-dish meal. And it's a superior comfort food, one that can warm you inside and out, and literally take care of you when you're sick.

A great soup recipe is one that you'll make again and again and keep forever. But there's a whole big world of soup; every country, every culture, every family has its traditional and well-loved recipes. With so many different soups out there, how do you find the keepers, the very best recipes to add to your repertoire? You look to *Cook's Illustrated*. We know a thing or two about making soup. Our test cooks have been making and testing soup recipes for more than 20 years. In this carefully curated collection, you'll find Italian Wedding Soup (page 63) and New England Clam Chowder (page 74) as well as Turkish Tomato, Bulgur, and Red Pepper Soup (page 26) and aromatic Provençal Fish Soup (page 38) for a taste of the Mediterranean. Foolproof versions of the classics are here too, from Ultimate French Onion Soup (page 106) and Hearty Minestrone (page 140) to Creamless Creamy Tomato Soup (page 123). We also put our test kitchen know-how to work when using no-prep chicken thighs to make the intense meaty broth for our Classic Chicken Noodle Soup (page 41) and oxtails to create deeply flavorful Beef Bone Broth (page 173), which can be used both for cooking and drinking (if you're into "souping").

This All-Time Best collection presents 75 recipes that we feel are our greatest contributions to the world of soup. Each has been tested over and over again until we came up with the "best" version; sometimes that meant making a recipe 30 to 50 times or more. What does that mean for you, the home cook? Recipes that you can trust and that are guaranteed to be interesting, full of flavor, and most importantly, foolproof.

Making a great pot of soup isn't hard, but it does require attention to detail, the right ingredients, well-made equipment, and a good recipe. *All-Time Best Soups* provides all of these things and more to support your efforts in the kitchen. Whether you want to learn how to make a homey chicken noodle soup from scratch, a quick weeknight beef and barley soup for dinner, a healthy super greens soup, or an elegant shrimp bisque for guests, *All-Time Best Soups* has you covered.

soup
basics

2 the test kitchen's all-time best tips for making soup
3 store-bought broths 101
4 defatting and pureeing soup
5 storing and reheating soup
6 stocking your kitchen
8 adding flavor to soup
9 serving soup
10 easiest-ever breads and homemade croutons

the test kitchen's all-time best tips for making soup

Soup might seem easy enough to make—but it's hard to hide mistakes in a pot (or bowl) of soup. To make sure every spoonful of soup is richly flavored, with juicy meat and tender vegetables, follow these test kitchen–tested tips.

use a sturdy pot It is worth investing in a heavy pot with a thick bottom to use for making soup. It will transfer heat evenly and prevent scorching, which can impart a burnt flavor to your soup. See our favorite Dutch oven and stockpot on page 6.

sauté the aromatics The first step in making many soups is to sauté aromatic vegetables such as onions and garlic. Sautéing not only softens their texture so that there is no unwelcome crunch in the soup, it also tames any harsh flavors and develops more complex flavors in the process. Medium heat is usually a good temperature for sautéing.

start with good stock There are some soups, like Classic Chicken Noodle Soup (page 41) and Beef Barley Soup with Mushrooms and Thyme (page 58), in which the flavor of the stock takes center stage, so it's best to use homemade. In boldly flavored soups with more going on, like Tortilla Soup (page 45) and Vietnamese Beef Pho (page 67), good store-bought broth is a fine and convenient option. Differences among packaged broths are quite significant—some are pretty flavorful while others taste like salty dishwater, so shop carefully. See pages 167–174 for our recipes for homemade stocks and broths. See page 3 for more information about buying broth.

cut the vegetables the right size Most soups call for chunks of vegetables. Haphazardly cut vegetables will cook unevenly—some pieces will be underdone and crunchy while others may be mushy. Cutting the vegetables to the size specified in the recipe ensures that the pieces will all be perfectly cooked.

stagger the addition of vegetables When a soup contains a variety of vegetables, their addition to the pot must often be staggered to account for their varying cooking times. Hardy vegetables like potatoes and winter squash can withstand much more cooking than delicate asparagus or spinach.

simmer, don't boil There is a fine line between simmering and boiling, and it can make a big difference in your soups. A simmer is a restrained version of a boil; fewer bubbles break the surface, and they do so with less vigor. Simmering heats food through more gently and more evenly than boiling; boiling causes vegetables such as potatoes to break apart or fray at the edges, and it can toughen meat, too.

season just before serving
In general, we add salt, pepper, and other seasonings—such as delicate herbs and lemon juice—after cooking, just before serving. The saltiness of the stock and other ingredients, such as canned tomatoes and canned beans, can vary greatly, so it's always best to taste and adjust the seasoning once the soup is complete, just before ladling it into bowls for serving.

Even though broth tastes worlds better when you make it yourself, it's not always essential or practical to use homemade. Plus, the reality is that the majority of home cooks rely on store-bought broth for most recipes. When selecting store-bought broth, it's important to choose wisely since what you use can have a big impact on your final result. The test kitchen has done extensive tastings on store-bought broths; here's what we've learned.

chicken broth We prefer chicken broth to beef broth and vegetable broth for its stronger, cleaner flavor. While searching for the best commercial chicken broth, we discovered a few critical characteristics. First, we like broth with a lower sodium content—less than 700 milligrams per serving—because, when simmered, evaporation loss concentrates the broth's saltiness. Also, we like broth with a short ingredient list that includes flavor-boosting vegetables like carrots, celery, and onions. Our favorite is **Swanson Chicken Stock**.

vegetable broth We turn to store-bought vegetable broth for vegetarian soups or for vegetable soups that might be overwhelmed by the flavor of chicken broth alone. In fact, because commercial vegetable broths tend to be sweet, we'll often mix vegetable broth with chicken broth for the best flavor. The highest-ranked commercial broth in our taste tests was **Orrington Farms Vegan Chicken Flavored Broth Base & Seasoning**, a 6-ounce jar of powder that makes up to 28 cups of broth. This powdered broth is well-balanced, nicely savory, and fairly salty. **Swanson Certified Organic Vegetable Broth** is our runner-up. It is a ready-to-use liquid broth that comes in a 32-ounce carton and is more expensive per ounce.

clam juice When we need clam juice for seafood soups or chowders, we reach for commercially prepared juice, made by briefly steaming fresh clams in salted water and filtering the resulting broth before bottling. Our winner, **Bar Harbor Clam Juice**, hails from the shores of clam country in Maine and is available nationwide. It brings a bright and mineral-y flavor.

beef broth Historically we've found beef broths to be short on beefy flavor, but with a few flavor additives, beef broth can pull off a deeply flavored beef soup. We tasted different beef broths, stocks, and bases to find out which one would suitably stand in for homemade. Generally, you should note the ingredients on the label; we found that the best broths had flavor-amplifying ingredients, such as yeast extract and tomato paste, near the top of the list and included concentrated beef stock. Our winner is **Better Than Bouillon Beef Base**. This paste is economical, stores easily, and dissolves quickly in hot water.

freezing broth

Whether we're using homemade or store-bought broth, we frequently have some extras left after cooking. To save the leftover amount, we either store it in an airtight container in the refrigerator for up to four days or freeze it for up to three months using one of these methods.

for small amounts Pour the broth into ice cube trays. After the cubes have frozen, remove them and store them in a zipper-lock bag. Use cubes for pan sauces, stir-fry sauces, and vegetable braises.

for medium amounts Ladle the broth into nonstick muffin tins (each muffin cup will hold about one cup). After the broth has frozen, store the "cups" in a large zipper-lock bag. "Cups" are good for casseroles and braising/steaming/poaching liquid.

for large amounts Line a 4-cup measuring cup with a zipper-lock bag (it holds the bag open so you can use both hands to pour) and pour in the cooled broth. Seal the bag (double up if you wish) and lay it flat to freeze. This is a good option for soup, stew, rice, or gravy.

defatting soup Defatting a broth or soup is important if you don't want your final dish to look and taste greasy. There are four different ways to defat a liquid; the method you choose depends on the dish you are making and the equipment you have on hand. For the first three methods, it is important to let the liquid settle for 5 to 10 minutes before defatting; this allows all of the fat to separate out and float to the top.

skim with a ladle or wide, shallow spoon This is the simplest way to defat a liquid. Let the liquid settle in the pot for 5 to 10 minutes, then skim away the fat with a wide spoon or ladle. The advantage of this method is that it's very easy and it doesn't dirty any extra dishes; however, some fat will remain in the broth.

use a tall, narrow container If you are using a large pot or have a large quantity of fat to skim, pour the broth into a tall, narrow container before defatting. This will create a deeper layer of fat that is easier to skim and remove. After letting the broth settle for 5 to 10 minutes, skim with a wide spoon or ladle. (Although some fat will remain behind, there will be less than if you simply defat the broth right in the pot.) This method works with all kinds of broths and soups.

use a fat separator This technique works best with broths that don't have much in the way of vegetables taking up space in the pot and requires a fat separator (see page 7 for our recommendation). To use, simply pour the liquid into the fat separator and let it settle for 5 to 10 minutes. Then pour it back into the pot through the spout, leaving the fat behind.

refrigerate overnight If you have time, you can refrigerate your broth overnight without defatting—the fat will collect and solidify on the top as it chills. Upon removing it from the refrigerator, you can simply scrape the large solid pieces of fat right off the top before reheating and using.

pureeing soup A pureed soup's texture should be as smooth and creamy as possible. With this in mind, we tried pureeing several soups with a food processor, a handheld immersion blender, and a regular countertop blender. We found that a standard blender turns out the smoothest soups. A food processor does a decent job of pureeing, but some small bits of vegetables can get trapped under the blade and remain unchopped. The immersion blender has appeal because it is brought to the pot, but we found that this kind of blender can leave unblended bits of food behind.

The blade on a standard blender does an excellent job with soups because it pulls ingredients down from the top of the container so no stray bits go untouched by the blade. And as long as plenty of headroom is left at the top of the blender, there is no leakage. Blending hot soup can be dangerous. To prevent a mess, blend the soup in batches and make sure the blender is filled only two-thirds full (or less). Hold the lid securely in place with a dish towel and pulse several times before blending continuously.

storing and reheating soup

Many soups make a generous number of servings, making it convenient to stock your freezer with the leftovers so you can pull them out and reheat them whenever you like. In general, we recommend refrigerating delicate soups, including vegetable or brothy soups, for no more than two days. We recommend freezing broths or soups for no longer than one month. Here's the information you need to properly cool, store, and thaw your soups so they heat up just as flavorful as freshly made.

cooling and storing For safety reasons, the U.S. Food and Drug Administration (FDA) recommends cooling liquids to 70 degrees within the first 2 hours after cooking and 41 degrees within 4 hours after that. As tempting as it might seem, avoid transferring hot soup straight to the refrigerator. You may speed up the cooling process, but you'll also increase the fridge's internal temperature to unsafe levels, which is dangerous for all the other food stored there. We found that letting the soup cool on the countertop for an hour helps it drop to about 85 degrees; the soup can then be transferred to the fridge and it will come down to 41 degrees in about 4 hours and 30 minutes (well within the FDA's recommended range). If you don't have an hour to cool your soup, you can divide the hot soup into a number of storage containers to cool more quickly or you can cool down the whole pot with our tip at right.

We like to refrigerate or freeze soup in airtight plastic storage containers (**Snapware Airtight** are our favorite); remember to leave a little room at the top of the container(s) to prevent the lid(s) from popping off.

freezing soups with dairy or pasta Creamy soups and soups that have a pasta component simply don't freeze very well. The dairy curdles as it freezes and the pasta turns bloated and mushy. Instead, make and freeze the soup without the dairy or pasta component included. After you have thawed the soup and it has been heated through, either stir in the uncooked pasta and simmer until just tender or stir in the dairy and continue to heat gently until hot (do not let it boil).

thawing For safety reasons, we recommend thawing frozen soups and stews in the refrigerator, never at room temperature, for 24 to 48 hours. (That said, if you've forgotten to plan ahead, you can heat frozen soups directly on the stovetop or in the microwave, but the texture of meat and vegetables will suffer a bit.)

reheating We prefer to reheat large amounts of soup in a heavy pot on the stovetop. Bring the soup to a rolling boil and make sure to stir often to ensure the entire pot reaches the boiling point. If you use the microwave, avoid reheating in the same container used to refrigerate or freeze the soup. Instead, we recommend that you transfer the food to a microwave-safe dish that's somewhat larger than the storage container. Just be sure to cover the dish to prevent a mess. Make sure to stop and stir several times to ensure that the soup reheats evenly.

cooling a whole pot

To smartly and safely cool down a whole pot of soup, fill a large cooler or the sink with cold water and ice packs. Place the Dutch oven or stockpot in the cooler or sink until the contents register about 85 degrees, 30 to 45 minutes, stirring the pot occasionally to speed the chilling process. Refill the cooler or sink with cold water if necessary.

freezing single servings

Freezing soups in small amounts is handy when you only need one or two servings. Here's an easy way to freeze convenient single servings: Set out a number of 10- or 12-ounce paper cups for hot beverages and fill each with a portion of cooled soup (but not all the way to the top). Label, wrap well in plastic wrap, and freeze each cup. Whenever you want a quick cup of soup, remove serving(s) from the freezer, pop the soup into a microwave-safe bowl or mug, cover, and microwave until hot and ready to serve.

You don't need any specialized equipment to make good soups and broths at home. A sturdy, heavy-bottomed Dutch oven and a chef's knife go a long way. Here are the useful items we reach for again and again when making broth and soup in the test kitchen.

blender

A blender is the only tool that can blend all manner of liquid-y foods (whether hot or cold) to a smooth texture so it is the best for making pureed soups. A blender's design pulls ingredients down to the blade, so it yields a finer, smoother puree than you get from either a food processor or an immersion blender. Our winning blender is the **Vitamix 5200** and our best buy is the **Breville Hemisphere Control**.

dutch oven

Built for both stovetop and oven use, a Dutch oven is generally wider and shallower than a conventional stockpot. A good-quality heavy-bottomed Dutch oven conducts heat steadily and evenly. Use a pot that has a capacity of at least 6 quarts. Our favorite is the **Le Creuset 7¼-Quart Round French Oven**.

fine-mesh strainer

A fine-mesh strainer separates solids from liquid. A diameter of at least 6 inches and a deep, fine-mesh bowl are good qualities to look for as are sturdy construction and a stable bowl rest so you can really press down on the solids. We like the **CIA Masters Collection Fine-Mesh Strainer**.

ladle

A ladle is indispensable for serving soups. We prefer one with a 9- to 10-inch handle so it doesn't slide into the pot. The handle should be slightly offset—this allows for clean pouring. You can also use a ladle to defat stock. Our favorite is the **Rösle Hook Ladle with Pouring Rim**.

wide, shallow spoon

A spoon with a thin, shallow, stainless-steel bowl makes it easy to skim the fat or scum off the surface of broth and soup. The best spoons have a handle of at least 9 inches like our favorite, the **Rösle Basting Spoon with Hook Handle**.

wooden spoon

A wooden spoon is simple yet perfect for scraping up fond off the bottom of the pot and for stirring hot mixtures. It is also good for pressing on solids in a strainer to extract liquid. Our winner is the **SCI Bamboo Wood Cooking Spoon**.

fat separator

Homemade broth often contains a fair amount of fat. A fat separator makes defatting hot broth simple: Just pour the broth in the top, let it settle, and pour the defatted broth out of the spout, leaving the fat behind. Choose a fat separator with a large capacity (ideally 4 cups), an integrated strainer, and a wide mouth that makes for easy filling. Our favorite is the **Cuisipro Fat Separator**.

stockpot

This heavy 12-quart pot is useful for handling a variety of big jobs, from making a double batch of chicken broth to steaming lobsters for bisque. Our winning pot is made by **All-Clad** and our best buy is the **Cuisinart Chef's Classic Stainless 12-Quart Stock Pot**.

whisk

An all-purpose whisk is useful for mixing ingredients together and smoothing out any lumps. An 11-inch whisk can reach into deep pots and bowls and the tines should be sturdy and flexible but should not twist. We like the **OXO Good Grips 11-inch Balloon Whisk**.

meat cleaver

A cleaver comes in handy for difficult tasks such as chopping up bones for broth, cutting up lobster for bisque, or halving butternut squash. The best meat cleavers feature thick, heavy, razor-sharp blades and a perfectly balanced design. We recommend the **Global 6-inch Meat Cleaver** and the **LamsonSharp 7-inch Meat Cleaver**.

chef's knife

With a good chef's knife in hand you can prep vegetables for soups and cut up chicken for broth. Our favorite is the **Victorinox Swiss Army Fibrox Pro 8-Inch Chef's Knife**, which is lightweight, has a blade that's just the right length, and has a comfortable grip and nonslip handle.

adding flavor to soup

The test kitchen uses some key ingredients over and over again in our soup recipes. Here are some of our favorite ways to impart flavor to a pot of soup and repurpose leftovers in the process.

freezing flavorings

You can save time, prep, and money by stashing certain soup flavorings in your freezer to use at a later date.

garlic Mince garlic, combine with ½ teaspoon vegetable oil per clove, and freeze in heaping tea-spoons on baking sheet. Transfer to zipper-lock bag.

ginger Grate ginger (frozen whole ginger turns spongy), freeze in 1-teaspoon portions on baking sheet, and transfer to zipper-lock bag.

citrus zest Freeze in packed ½-teaspoon mounds on baking sheet; transfer to zipper-lock bag. Avoid using as garnish since color fades.

rescuing soup that's too thick or too thin

If your soup is too thick, grad-ually add more water, broth, canned tomatoes, or whatever liquid is appropriate. Remember to correct the seasoning before serving. If your soup is too thin, you can try adding bread to soak up some of the liquid and then pureeing the bread in the blender before adding it back to the soup. If your bean soup is too thin, try mashing some of the beans to thicken the liquid.

parmesan cheese In the test kitchen we save Parmesan rinds to add depth to soups like Hearty Minestrone (page 140) and Sicilian Chickpea and Escarole Soup (page 153). The rind is particularly good for seasoning because it's the part of the cheese where most of the bacteria and mold grow and, thus, is the source of strong aroma and flavor compounds. If you don't have a Parmesan rind, the rinds from Pecorino-Romano and Gruyère add comparable savory flavor. When you can no longer grate any cheese off the rind, store the rind in a zipper-lock bag in the freezer; cheese rinds will keep indefinitely (no need to thaw them before using).

bacon Uncooked bacon adds smoky flavor to many soups such as Split Pea and Ham Soup (page 163). Cooked bacon pulls double duty providing rendered fat in which to cook aromatics for another layer of flavor, as in Farmhouse Chicken Chowder (page 73); the crisp bacon bits are then used to garnish the finished soup. If you have a partial package of bacon left over you can freeze slices for later use. They can be frozen and thawed with virtually no noticeable change in quality. Coil up each slice individually (to prevent sticking and to minimize freezer burn), freeze on a plate, and then transfer to a zipper-lock freezer bag.

fresh herbs In the test kitchen, we use fresh herbs more often than dried. We use chopped herbs such as parsley, cilantro, chives, mint, fennel fronds, or dill to deliver a big hit of fresh flavor to soup whether stirred into the pot at the end of cooking or sprinkled over a bowlful to serve. You can save leftover fresh herbs by freezing them; freezing alters their texture but their flavors remain remarkably intact. Chop parsley, basil, tarragon, or cilantro; transfer by the spoonful to ice cube trays, top with water, and freeze. Once frozen, transfer the cubes to a zipper-lock bag. You can add frozen cubes directly to soups.

bay leaf Bay leaves are a key seasoning in many soups. We prefer dried bay leaves to fresh; they work just as well in long-cooked recipes, are cheaper, and will keep for three months in an airtight container in the freezer. We prefer Turkish bay leaves to those from California. The California bay leaf has a medicinal and potent eucalyptus-like flavor, but the Turkish bay leaf has a mild, green, and slightly clove-like flavor.

chicken fat The fat you skim off of chicken broth can be put in a clean container and saved for another use. The flavorful fat makes a great sub-stitute for butter or oil in a number of savory applications, such as sautéing aromatics, roasting root vegetables, and frying eggs. Store the fat in an air-tight container in the refrigerator for up to one month or in the freezer for up to six months, adding more fat as desired.

serving soup

Today soup is more likely to be ladled straight from the pot, since serving soup from a tureen or as a first course seems to have fallen out of favor. None-theless all kinds of bowls are called into service for serving soup—smaller 6-ounce bowls or cups for rich soups like white gazpacho or shrimp bisque; large, shallow bowls to showcase the seafood in fish soup or for hearty main-dish fare; broiler-safe crocks for French onion soup; or casual mugs for a cup of creamy tomato soup or clam chowder.

cold soups Serve cold soups such as Classic Gazpacho (page 110) in chilled bowls. You can put the soup in a large pitcher and use it to pour out to serve.

garnish it! Many soups lend themselves to a final topping that offers com-plementary flavor, texture, and color. For some soups, such as Tortilla Soup (page 45), the garnishes are an essential finishing step. Simple pureed soups, which are also monochromatic, really benefit from a colorful garnish or two. They can be everything from chopped vegetables (see below) to flavor enhancers such as cilantro cream, a splash of hot sauce, or a spoonful of bright pesto. You can add one or two garnishes to each bowl of soup before serving, or you can offer them separately so that diners can garnish their bowls to taste.

extra-virgin olive oil A simple drizzle of extra-virgin olive oil adds a final layer of rich flavor to many soups such as Provençal Fish Soup (page 38) and also makes a beautiful presentation. Balsamic vinegar does the same for Tuscan White Bean Soup (page 144).

vegetables Diced avocado, chopped tomato or cucumber, sliced radishes, fresh chiles, and sliced scallions all add color and freshness as garnishes.

yogurt and sour cream A dollop of plain yogurt or sour cream adds a tangy and cooling counterpart to flavorful soups like Curried Red Lentil Soup (page 30) and Black Bean Soup (page 158). Sometimes we dress up sour cream with fresh herbs, as in our Beet and Wheat Berry Soup with Dill Cream (page 102).

citrus Lemon or lime juice or wedges always add a final bright note to bean soups and spicy soups like Thai-Style Chicken Soup (page 52).

crumbled cheese Goat or blue cheese, cheddar, *queso fresco*, and Cotija all make for quick and savory toppings. We like crumbled blue cheese on our 11th-Hour Harvest Pumpkin Soup (page 34).

toasted nuts or seeds Chopped nuts such as walnuts or almonds along with sesame seeds add a complementary crunchy topping to creamy and Asian-style soups. Toasting the nuts and seeds brings out their full flavor.

croutons See page 11 for our recipes for homemade croutons.

Bread has long been a trusty sidekick to soup, whether it's in the form of croutons or oyster crackers scattered over the top of chowder or a warm roll or piece of bread to go alongside it. Here are a few quick and easy bread recipes (thanks to pizza dough) that help turn your bowl of soup into a meal.

easy dinner rolls Heat oven to 400 degrees. Cut 8 ounces pizza dough into 4 even pieces and roll into balls. Arrange on well-oiled baking sheet, brush lightly with olive oil, and sprinkle with salt and pepper. Bake until golden, about 20 minutes. Let cool on wire rack and serve warm. Makes 4. (This recipe can be doubled.)

easy garlic rolls Heat oven to 375 degrees. Mix ¼ cup olive oil, 1 large minced garlic clove, ½ teaspoon salt, and ¼ teaspoon pepper in bowl. Cut 2 pounds pizza dough into 10 pieces, roll loosely into balls, and arrange on parchment-lined baking sheet. Brush rolls with 1 beaten egg and bake until golden, 30 to 35 minutes, brushing rolls with garlic oil halfway through baking time. Let cool on wire rack and serve warm. Makes 10.

soft and cheesy breadsticks Heat oven to 400 degrees. Roll out 1 pound pizza dough on lightly floured counter into 12 by 6-inch rectangle. Cut dough crosswise into 1-inch-wide strips and lay on well-oiled rimmed baking sheet. Brush with 1½ tablespoons olive oil, sprinkle with ¼ cup grated Parmesan cheese, and season with salt and pepper. Bake until golden, about 20 minutes. Let cool on wire rack and serve warm. Makes 12.

rosemary-olive focaccia Heat oven to 400 degrees. Press 1 pound pizza dough into well-oiled 13 by 9-inch baking dish or 10-inch pie plate and dimple surface with your fingers. Brush dough liberally with extra-virgin olive oil and sprinkle with ¼ cup chopped olives, ½ teaspoon minced fresh rosemary, ½ teaspoon kosher salt, and ½ teaspoon pepper. Bake until golden brown, about 30 minutes. Let cool on wire rack and serve warm. Serves 6.

classic croutons

makes 3 cups

Either fresh or stale bread can be used in this recipe, although stale bread is easier to cut and crisps more quickly in the oven.

6 slices hearty white sandwich bread, crusts removed, cut into ½-inch cubes (3 cups)

3 tablespoons unsalted butter, melted, or extra-virgin olive oil

Salt and pepper

Adjust oven rack to middle position and heat oven to 350 degrees. Toss bread with melted butter, season with salt and pepper, and spread onto rimmed baking sheet. Bake until golden brown and crisp, 20 to 25 minutes, stirring halfway through baking. Let cool and serve. (Croutons can be stored at room temperature for up to 3 days.)

variations

garlic croutons

Whisk 1 minced garlic clove into melted butter before tossing with bread.

cinnamon-sugar croutons

These croutons pair best with sweet soups like Creamy Butternut Squash Soup (page 126).

Toss buttered bread with 6 teaspoons sugar and 1½ teaspoons ground cinnamon before baking.

buttery rye croutons

makes 1½ cups

These croutons are made in a skillet; they can be made ahead and stored in an airtight container for one week.

3 tablespoons unsalted butter

1 tablespoon olive oil

2 slices light rye bread, cut into ½-inch cubes (1½ cups)

Salt

Heat butter and oil in 10-inch skillet over medium heat until butter melts. Add bread cubes and cook, stirring frequently, until golden brown, about 10 minutes. Transfer croutons to paper towel–lined plate and season with salt to taste.

herbed croutons

makes 2½ cups

1 tablespoon unsalted butter

1 teaspoon minced fresh parsley

½ teaspoon minced fresh thyme

4 slices hearty white sandwich bread, cut into ½-inch cubes

Salt and pepper

Melt butter in 10-inch skillet over medium heat. Add parsley and thyme; cook, stirring constantly, for 20 seconds. Add bread cubes and cook, stirring frequently, until light golden brown, 5 to 10 minutes. Transfer croutons to paper towel–lined plate and season with salt and pepper to taste.

garlic toasts

makes 8 slices
Be sure to use a high-quality crusty bread, such as a baguette; do not use sliced sandwich bread.

8 (1-inch-thick) slices rustic bread

1 large garlic clove, peeled

3 tablespoons extra-virgin olive oil

Salt and pepper

Adjust oven rack 6 inches from broiler element and heat broiler. Spread bread out evenly over rimmed baking sheet and broil, flipping as needed, until well toasted on both sides, about 4 minutes. Briefly rub 1 side of each toast with garlic, drizzle with oil, and season with salt and pepper to taste. Serve.

weeknight
workhorses

15 weeknight chicken noodle soup
    weeknight chicken and rice soup
17 chicken and ramen soup
    beef and ramen soup
18 quick beef and barley soup
21 quick beef and vegetable soup
22 caldo verde
25 baby carrot bisque with goat cheese
26 turkish tomato, bulgur, and red pepper soup
29 spicy thai-style shrimp soup
30 curried red lentil soup
33 easy black bean soup with chorizo
    easy vegetarian black bean soup
34 11th-hour harvest pumpkin soup

why this recipe works With this fast recipe you can make a restorative bowl of chicken soup any time the need arises. We produced a quick-cooking soup with both a flavorful broth and tender chicken without the benefit of either homemade broth or a whole bird. Since we would be relying on store-bought broth, we had to find a way to augment its mild flavor. Heating the broth with bay leaves and thyme enlivened it and lent it a home-made taste. We also simmered the doctored broth with carrots and celery, so that it would spend time becoming infused with flavor. Next, we focused on the chicken. Boneless, skinless breasts were the obvious choice because of their short cooking time, but simply simmering cubes of meat in broth often leads to tough nuggets of chicken. We avoided this problem by browning split breasts in the pot, poaching them whole in the broth, and then shred-ding them once cooked. This way, the chicken remained moist and tender. Browning the chicken left behind flavorful browned bits, called fond, which helped build a complex and rich broth. For the best flavor, we cooked the egg noodles, or rice, right in the broth. Minced parsley added a final hit of freshness. See page 3 for more information on store-bought broth.

serves 6

6 cups chicken broth

1 teaspoon minced fresh thyme, or ¼ teaspoon dried

2 bay leaves

1 pound boneless, skinless chicken breasts, trimmed

Salt and pepper

1 tablespoon vegetable oil

1 onion, chopped fine

2 carrots, peeled and sliced ¼ inch thick

1 celery rib, sliced ¼ inch thick

3 ounces (2 cups) egg noodles

2 tablespoons minced fresh parsley

1. Microwave broth, thyme, and bay leaves in large liquid measuring cup until just boiling, 2 to 4 minutes. Meanwhile, pat chicken dry with paper towels and season with salt and pepper. Heat oil in Dutch oven over medium-high heat until just smoking. Brown chicken lightly on both sides, about 5 minutes; transfer to plate.

2. Add onion and ½ teaspoon salt to fat left in pot and cook over medium heat until lightly browned, about 5 minutes. Reduce heat to low and stir in hot broth mixture, scraping up any browned bits. Add carrots, celery, and browned chicken and any accumulated juices. Cover and simmer gently until chicken registers 160 degrees, about 10 minutes.

3. Transfer chicken to cutting board, let cool slightly, and shred into bite-size pieces. Stir noodles into soup, increase heat to medium-high, and simmer until just tender, 5 to 8 minutes. Off heat, discard bay leaves and stir in shredded chicken and parsley. Season with salt and pepper to taste, and serve.

variation

weeknight chicken and rice soup
Omit egg noodles. Add 1½ cups long-grain rice to pot with vege-tables and browned chicken in step 2. After removing chicken in step 3, increase heat to medium-high and cook until rice is tender, about 5 minutes.

chicken and ramen soup

why this recipe works This quick Asian-style noodle soup is built around a full-flavored broth. To keep it easy, we used the noodles from store-bought ramen soup, discarding the seasoning packet, which tasted dusty and was too salty. Store-bought coleslaw mix conveniently provided already shredded cabbage (and carrots) ready to add to the pot. Ginger, soy sauce, and sesame oil added significant savoriness to our otherwise simple soup. Gently poaching boneless chicken breasts in the broth and then shredding the meat before returning it to the soup kept the meat tender and flavorful. Be careful not to overcook the chicken in step 3 or it will taste dry. You can find shredded coleslaw mix in the packaged salad aisle at the grocery store.

serves 4 to 6

1 tablespoon vegetable oil

1 pound boneless, skinless chicken breasts, trimmed

Salt and pepper

5 scallions, white and green parts separated and sliced thin

2 tablespoons grated fresh ginger

2 garlic cloves, minced

6 cups chicken broth

2 tablespoons dry sherry

2 tablespoons soy sauce, plus extra as needed

2 (3-ounce) packages ramen noodles, flavoring packets discarded

3 cups shredded coleslaw mix

3 ounces (3 cups) baby spinach

1 tablespoon sesame oil, plus extra as needed

1. Heat vegetable oil in Dutch oven over medium-high heat until just smoking. Pat chicken dry with paper towels and season with salt and pepper. Brown chicken lightly on both sides, about 5 minutes; transfer to plate.

2. Add scallion whites, ginger, and garlic to fat left in pot and cook over medium heat until fragrant, about 1 minute. Stir in broth, sherry, and soy sauce, scraping up any browned bits.

3. Add browned chicken, cover, and simmer gently until it registers 160 degrees, about 10 minutes. Transfer chicken to cutting board and shred into bite-size pieces.

4. Meanwhile, return soup to simmer, stir in noodles and coleslaw mix, and cook until noodles are tender, about 4 minutes. Stir in shredded chicken and spinach and cook until spinach is wilted, about 1 minute. Stir in scallion greens and sesame oil. Season with salt, pepper, soy sauce, and sesame oil to taste. Serve.

variation

beef and ramen soup

To make the beef easier to slice, freeze it for 15 minutes. Do not overcook the beef once it is added to the soup or it will taste tough and dry.

Substitute 1 pound flank steak, sliced ¼ inch thick against grain then cut crosswise into bite-size pieces, for chicken. For broth, use 3 cups beef broth and 3 cups chicken broth. Skip step 1 and heat oil in pot over medium heat until shimmering before adding scallion whites, ginger, and garlic. Add raw beef, noodles, and coleslaw mix to soup together in step 4; cook until beef is no longer pink and noodles are tender, about 4 minutes, before adding spinach.

why this recipe works This meaty and rich soup lets the star ingredients—beef and barley—shine through. Beef barley soup usually takes some time to make; to speed things up we turned to sirloin steak tips, a cut that is already tender and full of flavor. By cutting the meat into ¼-inch pieces, we were able to brown it in a skillet while the soup base simmered and then stir it in at the end to cook through quickly. Since beef broth can add a tinny flavor, we mixed it with an equal amount of chicken broth, which created the perfect foundation for our quick and hearty soup. Enhancing the broths with sautéed aromatics, porcini, tomato paste, and soy sauce took our soup to the next level. Look for whole steak tips (sometimes labeled flap meat) rather than those that have been cut into small pieces for stir-fries. Be careful not to overcook the beef in step 3 or it will taste dry.

serves 4 to 6

3 carrots, peeled and cut into
¼-inch pieces

1 onion, chopped fine

¼ cup olive oil

1 tablespoon minced fresh
thyme or 1 teaspoon dried

¼ ounce dried porcini
mushrooms, rinsed and minced

2 garlic cloves, minced

2 teaspoons tomato paste

3 cups beef broth

3 cups chicken broth

⅔ cup quick-cooking barley

2 teaspoons soy sauce

1½ pounds sirloin steak tips,
trimmed and cut into ½-inch
pieces

Salt and pepper

1. Combine carrots, onion, and 2 tablespoons oil in Dutch oven and cook over medium-high heat until vegetables are softened and lightly browned, about 8 minutes. Stir in thyme, porcini, garlic, and tomato paste and cook until fragrant, about 30 seconds. Stir in beef broth, chicken broth, barley, and soy sauce, scraping up any browned bits. Simmer until barley is tender, about 15 minutes.

2. Meanwhile, heat 1 tablespoon oil in 12-inch skillet over medium-high heat until just smoking. Pat beef dry with paper towels and season with salt and pepper. Brown half of beef on all sides, about 8 minutes; transfer to bowl. Repeat with remaining 1 tablespoon oil and remaining beef; transfer to bowl.

3. Add browned beef and any accumulated juices to soup and let heat through, about 1 minute. Season with salt and pepper to taste. Serve.

quick beef and vegetable soup

why this recipe works This easy recipe lets you get a family-pleasing hearty bowl of meat and vegetable soup on the table in record time. To make this classic soup for dinner any night of the week, we found that quick-cooking ground beef was a great alternative to beef cubes for a meaty, satisfying soup that's ready in half an hour. Not only is ground beef easy to find and relatively inexpensive but just 1 pound of it gives a lot of bang for the buck. The meat broke apart as it browned and released its flavor quickly. Cutting the fresh vegetables into small pieces sped up their cooking time and meant we didn't need to resort to using frozen ones, while canned diced tomatoes conveniently added fresh tomato flavor to our soup. You can substitute chicken broth for the beef broth if you prefer.

serves 4

1 pound 90 percent lean ground beef

1 onion, chopped

2 carrots, peeled and cut into ½-inch pieces

1 teaspoon dried oregano

Salt and pepper

4 cups beef broth

1 (14.5-ounce) can diced tomatoes

8 ounces Yukon Gold potatoes, peeled and cut into ½-inch pieces

6 ounces green beans, trimmed and cut on bias into 1-inch lengths

2 tablespoons chopped fresh parsley

1. Cook beef, onion, carrots, oregano, 1 teaspoon salt, and ½ teaspoon pepper in Dutch oven over medium-high heat, breaking up beef with spoon until no longer pink, about 6 minutes. Add broth, tomatoes and their juice, and potatoes. Bring to boil, reduce heat to low, and simmer, covered, until potatoes are almost tender, about 10 minutes.

2. Add green beans and cook, uncovered, until vegetables are tender and soup has thickened slightly, 10 to 12 minutes. Season with salt and pepper to taste. Sprinkle with parsley and serve.

caldo verde

why this recipe works Everything about *caldo verde*, the classic Portuguese soup of smoky sausage, potato, and hearty greens, is quick-cooking, hearty, and satisfying. Its thin broth is usually made with just water, but for our version we added chicken broth for deeper flavor. We then realized that we could further improve the broth by pureeing some of the softened potatoes with a few tablespoons of olive oil to thicken up the broth and add richness and body. We used lower-starch Yukon Gold potatoes, which held their shape. Increasing the amount of potato and garlicky sausage turned this simple soup into a filling meal, while a bit of white wine vinegar brightened up the pot. We prefer collard greens for their delicate sweetness and meatier bite, but kale can be substituted. Serve this soup with hearty bread and, for added richness, a final drizzle of extra-virgin olive oil.

serves 6 to 8

1/4 cup extra-virgin olive oil

12 ounces Spanish-style chorizo sausage, cut into 1/2-inch pieces

1 onion, chopped fine

4 garlic cloves, minced

Salt and pepper

1/4 teaspoon red pepper flakes

2 pounds Yukon Gold potatoes, peeled and cut into 3/4-inch pieces

4 cups chicken broth

4 cups water

1 pound collard greens, stemmed and cut into 1-inch pieces

2 teaspoons white wine vinegar

1. Heat 1 tablespoon oil in Dutch oven over medium-high heat until shimmering. Add chorizo and cook, stirring occasionally, until lightly browned, 4 to 5 minutes. Transfer chorizo to bowl and set aside. Reduce heat to medium and add onion, garlic, 1 1/4 teaspoons salt, and pepper flakes and season with pepper to taste. Cook, stirring frequently, until onion is translucent, 2 to 3 minutes. Add potatoes, broth, and water; increase heat to high and bring to boil. Reduce heat to medium-low and simmer, uncovered, until potatoes are just tender, 8 to 10 minutes.

2. Transfer 3/4 cup solids and 3/4 cup broth to blender. Add collard greens to pot and simmer for 10 minutes. Stir in chorizo and continue to simmer until greens are tender, 8 to 10 minutes longer.

3. Add remaining 3 tablespoons oil to soup in blender and process until very smooth and homogeneous, about 1 minute. Remove pot from heat and stir pureed soup mixture and vinegar into soup. Season with salt and pepper to taste, and serve.

why this recipe works You can pull off this elegant bisque in short order—no peeling or chopping required—by reaching for fuss-free baby carrots. Simmering the carrots in broth took just 20 minutes. Chicken broth alone made the soup too chicken-y while just vegetable broth made it too sweet, but using an equal amount of both chicken and vegetable broths provided a balanced sweet and savory flavor profile. Coriander and thyme added a pleasant aroma without overwhelming the delicate carrot flavor. After quickly pureeing the soup in a blender, we added just ½ cup of half-and-half to make it rich and creamy. If your baby carrots are particularly thick, they may require a longer simmering time in step 2 to become tender. Of course, you can substitute regular carrots, peeled and cut into 1-inch pieces, for the baby carrots here. Crumbled goat cheese and minced chives make a savory and pretty-looking garnish for this soup.

serves 4 to 6

2 tablespoons vegetable oil

1½ pounds baby carrots

1 onion, chopped

2 garlic cloves, minced

1 teaspoon minced fresh thyme or ¼ teaspoon dried

½ teaspoon ground coriander

2½ cups chicken broth, plus extra as needed

2½ cups vegetable broth

½ cup half-and-half

Salt and pepper

1 tablespoon minced fresh chives

3 ounces goat cheese, crumbled (¾ cup)

1. Combine oil, carrots, and onion in Dutch oven and cook over medium-high heat until vegetables are softened, about 5 minutes. Stir in garlic, thyme, and coriander and cook until fragrant, about 30 seconds.

2. Stir in chicken broth and vegetable broth and bring to boil. Cover, reduce heat to medium-low, and simmer gently until carrots are tender, about 20 minutes.

3. Working in batches, process soup in blender until smooth, about 2 minutes. Return soup to clean pot and stir in half-and-half. Add extra chicken broth as needed to adjust soup's consistency. Heat soup gently over low heat until hot (do not boil). Season with salt and pepper to taste. Sprinkle individual portions with chives and goat cheese before serving.

turkish tomato, bulgur, and red pepper soup

why this recipe works This enticing tomato and red pepper soup is our take on the countless versions found throughout Turkey, all of which are full-flavored, enriched with grains, and simple to make. We started with onion and red bell peppers, softening them before we created a solid flavor backbone with garlic, dried mint, smoked paprika, and red pepper flakes. For additional smokiness, canned fire-roasted tomatoes did the trick. For the grain, we turned to versatile bulgur. While it plays an important role in innumerable salads, bulgur also has a place in making soups. When stirred into our soup, the bulgur absorbed the surrounding flavors and gave off starch that created a silky texture. Since bulgur is so quick-cooking, we stirred it in toward the end, giving it just enough time to become tender. A sprinkle of fresh mint gave the soup a final punch of flavor.

serves 6 to 8

2 tablespoons extra-virgin olive oil

1 onion, chopped

2 red bell peppers, stemmed, seeded, and chopped

Salt and pepper

3 garlic cloves, minced

1 teaspoon dried mint

½ teaspoon smoked paprika

⅛ teaspoon red pepper flakes

1 tablespoon tomato paste

½ cup dry white wine

1 (28-ounce) can diced fire-roasted tomatoes

4 cups vegetable broth

2 cups water

¾ cup medium-grind bulgur, rinsed

⅓ cup chopped fresh mint

1. Heat oil in Dutch oven over medium heat until shimmering. Add onion, bell peppers, ¾ teaspoon salt, and ¼ teaspoon pepper and cook until softened and beginning to brown, 6 to 8 minutes. Stir in garlic, dried mint, smoked paprika, and pepper flakes and cook until fragrant, about 30 seconds. Stir in tomato paste and cook for 1 minute.

2. Stir in wine, scraping up any browned bits, and simmer until reduced by half, about 1 minute. Add tomatoes and cook, stirring occasionally, until tomatoes soften and begin to break apart, about 10 minutes.

3. Stir in broth, water, and bulgur and bring to simmer. Reduce heat to low, cover, and cook until bulgur is tender, about 20 minutes. Season with salt and pepper to taste. Sprinkle individual portions with fresh mint and serve.

spicy thai-style shrimp soup

why this recipe works This quick Thai-style soup possesses a unique freshness and offers exotic flavors by way of grocery store ingredients. Based on a soup called *tom yum*, our shrimp soup has just the right balance of hot, salty, sweet, and sour elements. We substituted easy-to-find jalapeño peppers for traditional Thai chiles, while fish sauce provided the saltiness. The soup's sourness authentically comes from a combination of lemon grass and kaffir lime leaves, which we replaced with lime juice added to the soup at the last minute. Plain white sugar, a substitute for palm sugar, helped balance the chile heat, fish sauce saltiness, and sourness. Feel free to add a stalk of lemon grass to the broth, trimmed of its fibrous top and bruised with the flat side of a knife. For maximum heat, do not seed the chiles.

serves 4 to 6

5¼ cups chicken broth

1 (½-inch) piece fresh ginger, cut in half and smashed

2 large garlic cloves, lightly crushed with skins on

2 tablespoons fish sauce

4–6 cilantro stems, including roots, plus ¼ cup coarsely chopped fresh cilantro

1 teaspoon sugar

2 medium jalapeño chiles, stemmed, seeded, and sliced crosswise into ¼-inch rings

2 medium tomatoes, cored and chopped coarse

8 ounces cremini, oyster, or white mushrooms, stemmed and quartered if small or cut into sixths if large

8 ounces medium shrimp (41 to 50 per pound), peeled, deveined, and tails removed

3 tablespoons lime juice (2 limes)

1. Bring broth, ginger, garlic, fish sauce, cilantro stems, sugar, half of chiles, and one-quarter of tomatoes to boil in large saucepan over medium-high heat. Reduce heat to low and simmer for 20 minutes. Strain broth through fine-mesh strainer set over large bowl, pushing on solids to extract as much liquid as possible.

2. Return broth to pan and bring to simmer over medium-high heat. Add mushrooms and remaining chiles and cook for 2 minutes. Add shrimp and cook for 1 minute longer. Off heat, add lime juice. Evenly portion remaining tomato and chopped cilantro among individual bowls and ladle soup over top. Serve immediately.

to make ahead
The broth (through step 1) can be prepared up to 2 days in advance. Just remember to withhold the lime juice until the last moment; otherwise, its flavor and aroma will dissipate.

curried red lentil soup

why this recipe works Small red lentils are one of our favorite legumes; they do not hold their shape when cooked but break down into a creamy, thick puree—perfect for a hearty, satisfying soup. Lentils are popular in quick-cooking soups because of their short cooking time and the fact that they don't require soaking before cooking. To speed things up even further, we precooked the lentils in the microwave while we assembled the soup base. The mild flavor of the lentils did require some embellishment, which we achieved thanks to curry powder and fresh ginger. Sautéing the curry powder with garlic and the ginger before adding the lentils and the broth was key, as it intensified and deepened their flavors. Chopped fresh tomato enlivened the soup and added some complexity. Do not substitute brown lentils for the red lentils here; brown lentils have a very different texture.

serves 4

1 cup red lentils, picked over and rinsed

4 cups vegetable broth

2 tablespoons unsalted butter

1 onion, chopped fine

3 garlic cloves, minced

1 tablespoon grated fresh ginger

1 tablespoon curry powder

1 large tomato, cored, seeded, and cut into ¼-inch pieces

Salt and pepper

2 tablespoons minced fresh cilantro

½ cup plain yogurt

1. Microwave lentils and 2 cups broth in bowl until lentils are nearly tender and most liquid is absorbed, about 8 minutes.

2. Meanwhile, melt butter in Dutch oven over medium heat. Add onion and cook until softened, about 5 minutes. Stir in garlic, ginger, and curry powder and cook until fragrant, about 30 seconds.

3. Stir in microwaved lentil mixture, tomato, and remaining 2 cups broth and simmer until lentils are very tender and flavors meld, about 15 minutes. Season with salt and pepper to taste. Sprinkle individual portions with cilantro and dollop with yogurt before serving.

easy black bean soup with chorizo

why this recipe works This black bean soup is great for a weeknight because it takes just about an hour to make. We avoided the long process of soaking and simmering dried black beans by going straight for canned. Pureeing a portion of the beans gave our soup body, while a hearty base of aromatics—garlic, oregano, cumin, and chili powder—gave it a lot of flavor. For the liquid, chicken broth proved the best bet because its flavor was not intrusive. Since the soup is cooked so briefly, we looked for a quick-cooking pork product and found that sliced spicy chorizo sausage added meaty richness. We preferred to top our bowls of this soup with the simple and classic garnishes of sour cream, a sprinkle of cilantro, and lime wedges.

serves 4 to 6

4 (15-ounce) cans black beans, rinsed

3 cups chicken broth

1 tablespoon vegetable oil

6 ounces chorizo sausage, halved lengthwise and sliced ¼ inch thick

1 onion, chopped fine

1 red bell pepper, stemmed, seeded, and chopped fine

6 garlic cloves, minced

1 tablespoon minced fresh oregano or 1 teaspoon dried

½ teaspoon ground cumin

½ teaspoon chili powder

½ cup minced fresh cilantro

Salt and pepper

Hot sauce

1. Process 2 cups beans and 1 cup broth in blender until smooth, about 10 seconds; set aside.

2. Combine oil, chorizo, onion, and bell pepper in Dutch oven and cook over medium-high heat until vegetables are softened and lightly browned, 5 to 7 minutes. Stir in garlic, oregano, cumin, and chili powder and cook until fragrant, about 30 seconds. Stir in remaining 2 cups broth, scraping up any browned bits.

3. Stir in pureed beans and remaining beans and simmer until flavors meld, about 15 minutes. Stir in cilantro and season with salt, pepper, and hot sauce to taste. Serve.

variation

easy vegetarian black bean soup
Substitute 3 cups vegetable broth for chicken broth and omit chorizo. Add ¼ ounce dried porcini mushrooms, rinsed and minced, to pot with garlic, oregano, and spices.

11th-hour harvest pumpkin soup

why this recipe works This velvety pumpkin soup is surprisingly easy and fast thanks to canned pumpkin. The trick is getting rich, balanced pumpkin flavor out of a can. We started by creating a deeply flavorful base for our soup by softening onion and then adding cumin, coriander, and nutmeg, which gave us a warm-spiced flavor that paired well with pumpkin. Maple syrup was the ideal sweetener, adding depth and enhancing the nuttiness of the soup without overwhelming it with sweetness. A combination of vegetable broth and water gave the soup a subtle savory backbone, and just a half cup of half-and-half gave us an ideal creamy texture. Briefly simmering the pumpkin in the flavorful liquid allowed the flavors to meld and cooked off the tinny flavor of the canned pumpkin; we then pureed the soup to a silky consistency. Be sure to buy pure canned pumpkin, not pumpkin pie filling, which has sugar and spices added. Crumbled blue cheese and toasted, chopped walnuts make nice garnishes to this soup.

serves 4 to 6

2 tablespoons unsalted butter

1 onion, minced

2 garlic cloves, minced

½ teaspoon ground cumin

½ teaspoon ground coriander

¼ teaspoon ground nutmeg

3 cups vegetable broth, plus extra as needed

2 cups water

1 (15-ounce) can unsweetened pumpkin puree

¼ cup maple syrup

½ cup half-and-half

Salt and pepper

1. Melt butter in Dutch oven over medium heat. Add onion and cook until softened, about 5 minutes. Stir in garlic, cumin, coriander, and nutmeg and cook until fragrant, about 30 seconds.

2. Stir in broth, water, pumpkin, and maple syrup, scraping up any browned bits, and bring to boil. Reduce to simmer and cook until flavors have melded, about 15 minutes.

3. Working in batches, process soup in blender until smooth, 1 to 2 minutes. Return pureed soup to clean pot and stir in half-and-half; adjust consistency with additional broth as needed. Heat soup gently over low heat until hot (do not boil). Season with salt and pepper to taste, and serve.

soups from
around
the world

38 provençal fish soup
41 classic chicken noodle soup
42 matzo ball soup
45 tortilla soup
46 hearty cream of chicken soup
48 mexican-style chicken and chickpea soup
51 italian chicken soup with parmesan dumplings
52 thai-style chicken soup
55 mulligatawny with chicken
57 spicy moroccan-style lamb and lentil soup (harira)
58 beef barley soup with mushrooms and thyme
    beef noodle soup with mushrooms and thyme
60 mexican beef and vegetable soup
63 italian wedding soup
64 russian-style beef and cabbage soup
67 vietnamese beef pho
69 ramen soup with pork

provençal fish soup

why this recipe works This Provence-inspired fish soup is not only easy to make, it also boasts a richly flavored broth thanks to the combination of fragrant fennel, paprika, saffron, and orange zest. For the fish we chose thick cuts of cod loin, wanting a firm fish that would not break apart too easily. The problem then came in building the soup base. Initial tests with premade fish stock produced soups that overpowered the cod's own mild flavor. On the other extreme, water-based versions were more delicate in flavor but lacked any real depth or richness. Deglazing the vegetables and spices with wine and bottled clam juice helped to bring out a more balanced flavor, but tasters wanted even more body. So we browned a small amount of pancetta and cooked the vegetables in the fat. We loved this version, noting a perfect blend of smokiness, richness, and citrus aroma. Now all we had to do was cook the fish perfectly. Instead of cutting the cod into chunks, we left the fish in big slices so that they wouldn't break apart too much when stirred. We tried simmering the fish over low heat, but each time we employed direct heat, the fish was overcooked by the time it was served. We decided on a more unconventional method: We placed the fish in the pot, shut off the heat, and let it poach gently. This technique was undeniably successful: The fish was perfectly cooked. Finally, we had a hearty, fragrant fish soup with perfect broth and perfect fish.

serves 6 to 8

1 tablespoon extra-virgin olive oil, plus extra for drizzling

6 ounces pancetta, chopped fine

1 fennel bulb, 2 tablespoons fronds minced, stalks discarded, bulb halved, cored, and cut into 1/2-inch pieces

1 onion, chopped

2 celery ribs, halved lengthwise and cut into 1/2-inch pieces

4 garlic cloves, minced

Salt and pepper

1 teaspoon paprika

1/8 teaspoon red pepper flakes

Pinch saffron threads, crumbled

1 cup dry white wine or vermouth

4 cups water

2 (8-ounce) bottles clam juice

2 bay leaves

2 pounds skinless cod fillets, 1 to 1 1/2 inches thick, sliced crosswise into 6 equal pieces

2 tablespoons minced fresh parsley

1 tablespoon grated orange zest

1. Heat oil in Dutch oven over medium heat until shimmering. Add pancetta and cook, stirring occasionally, until meat is browned and fat is rendered, about 6 minutes. Add fennel bulb, onion, and celery, and cook until vegetables are softened and lightly browned, 12 to 14 minutes.

2. Stir in garlic, 1 1/2 teaspoons salt, paprika, pepper flakes, and saffron, and cook until fragrant, about 30 seconds. Stir in wine, scraping up any browned bits. Add water, clam juice, and bay leaves, bring to simmer, and cook until flavors meld, 15 to 20 minutes.

3. Off heat, discard bay leaves, place cod fillets in cooking liquid, cover, and let sit until fish flakes apart when gently prodded with paring knife and registers 140 degrees, 8 to 10 minutes. Add parsley, fennel fronds, and orange zest and stir gently with wooden spoon to break fish into large pieces. Season with salt and pepper to taste. Serve, drizzling individual portions with oil.

why this recipe works This classic rendition of chicken soup starts the old-fashioned way, by making a from-scratch broth. But instead of using a whole chicken we turned to meaty chicken thighs, which kept things easier; they also added intense, meaty flavor to the broth. To cut down on greasiness, we removed the skin after browning and before letting the thighs simmer along with the chopped and sautéed onion and bay leaves. Since most people prefer white meat in their chicken soup, we simply poached two boneless, skinless chicken breasts in the simmering broth, removing them when tender to add to the soup at the end. With the broth and the meat taken care of, we turned our attention to the soup with an eye toward keeping things simple and traditional. Onion, carrot, and celery and some fresh thyme fit the bill. As for the noodles, cooking them right in the broth intensified their flavor. Note that the thighs are used to flavor the broth, but once the broth is strained, the meat can be shredded and used for chicken salad or a pot pie. If you prefer dark meat in your soup, you can omit the chicken breasts and add the shredded thigh meat to the soup instead.

serves 8 to 10

broth
4 pounds bone-in, skin-on chicken thighs, trimmed

Salt and pepper

1 tablespoon vegetable oil

1 onion, chopped

12 cups water

2 bay leaves

1 pound boneless, skinless chicken breasts, trimmed

soup
1 tablespoon vegetable oil

1 onion, chopped fine

1 carrot, peeled and sliced thin

1 celery rib, halved lengthwise and sliced thin

2 teaspoons minced fresh thyme

6 ounces wide egg noodles

¼ cup minced fresh parsley

Salt and pepper

1. for the broth Pat thighs dry with paper towels and season with salt and pepper. Heat oil in Dutch oven over medium-high heat until smoking. Cook half of thighs skin side down until deep golden brown, about 6 minutes. Turn thighs and lightly brown second side, about 2 minutes. Transfer to strainer set in large bowl. Repeat with remaining thighs and transfer to strainer; discard fat in bowl. Pour off fat from pot, add onion, and cook over medium heat until just softened, about 3 minutes. Meanwhile, remove and discard skin from thighs. Add thighs, water, bay leaves, and 1 tablespoon salt to pot. Cover and simmer for 30 minutes. Add chicken breasts and continue simmering until broth is rich and flavorful, about 15 minutes.

2. Strain broth into large container, let stand for at least 10 minutes, then remove fat from surface. Meanwhile, transfer chicken to cutting board to cool. Once cooled, remove thigh meat from bones,

shred, and reserve for another use (can refrigerate for up to 2 days or freeze for up to 1 month). Shred breast meat and reserve for soup.

3. for the soup Heat oil in now-empty Dutch oven over medium-high heat until shimmering. Add onion, carrot, and celery and cook until onion has softened, 3 to 4 minutes. Stir in thyme and broth and simmer until vegetables are tender, about 15 minutes. Add noodles and shredded breast meat and simmer until noodles are just tender, about 5 minutes. Off heat, stir in parsley and season with salt and pepper. Serve.

to make ahead
Cooled broth and shredded breast meat can be refrigerated separately for up to 2 days or frozen for up to 1 month before being used to make soup. To avoid soggy noodles and vegetables, finish soup (step 3 in recipe) just before you plan on serving it.

matzo ball soup

why this recipe works Matzo ball soup can be controversial, but there is no question that this version hits all the marks, delivering tender dumplings and a savory broth. For matzo balls that were substantial but not too heavy or greasy we settled on a ratio of 1 cup matzo meal to 4 eggs and 5 tablespoons of water, plus a bit of chopped, cooked onion and minced dill. For the soup, we turned to the classic *mirepoix* ingredients plus parsnip for a touch of sweetness. To deepen the broth's chicken flavor, we added two whole chicken legs, which we removed after they cooked through. (The meat may be added back in if you like.) Chicken fat, or schmaltz, is available in the refrigerator or freezer section of most supermarkets. Note that the matzo batter needs to be refrigerated for at least 1 hour before shaping.

serves 6

matzo balls
¼ cup chicken fat (schmaltz) or vegetable oil

1 onion, chopped fine

4 large eggs

1 teaspoon minced fresh dill

Salt and pepper

1 cup (4 ounces) matzo meal

soup
1 tablespoon chicken fat (schmaltz) or vegetable oil

1 onion, chopped

2 carrots, peeled and cut into ½-inch chunks

2 celery ribs, chopped

1 parsnip, peeled and cut into ½-inch chunks

Salt and pepper

8 cups chicken broth

1½ pounds chicken leg quarters, trimmed

1 teaspoon minced fresh dill

1. for the matzo balls Heat chicken fat in Dutch oven over medium heat until shimmering. Add onion and cook until light golden brown and softened, about 5 minutes. Transfer onion to large bowl and let cool for 10 minutes. (Do not clean pot.)

2. Whisk eggs, 5 tablespoons water, dill, ¾ teaspoon salt, and ½ teaspoon pepper into cooled onion. Fold in matzo meal until well combined. Cover with plastic wrap and refrigerate for at least 1 hour or up to 2 hours. (Batter will thicken as it sits.)

3. Bring 4 quarts water and 2 tablespoons salt to boil in now-empty Dutch oven. Divide batter into 12 portions (about 1 heaping tablespoon each) and place on greased plate. Roll portions into smooth balls between your wet hands and return to plate. Transfer matzo balls to boiling water, cover, reduce heat to medium-low, and simmer until tender and cooked through, about 30 minutes.

4. Using slotted spoon, transfer matzo balls to colander and drain briefly. Transfer balls to clean plate and let cool to firm up, about 10 minutes. Discard cooking water. (Do not clean pot.)

5. for the soup Meanwhile, heat chicken fat in large saucepan over medium heat until shimmering. Add onion, carrots, celery, parsnip, and ½ teaspoon salt and cook, covered, until vegetables begin to soften, about 5 minutes. Add broth, chicken, and dill and bring to boil. Cover, reduce heat to low, and cook until chicken is tender, 35 to 45 minutes. Remove from heat and transfer chicken to plate. (Chicken can be used for soup or reserved for another use. If adding to soup, shred with 2 forks into bite-size pieces; discard skin and bones.) Season soup with salt and pepper to taste.

6. Transfer soup to now-empty Dutch oven and bring to simmer over medium heat. Carefully transfer matzo balls to hot soup (along with shredded chicken, if using). Cover and cook until matzo balls are heated through, about 5 minutes. Serve.

to make ahead
Soup and matzo balls can be fully cooked, cooled, and refrigerated separately for up to 2 days. To serve, return soup to simmer over medium heat, add matzo balls, and cook until heated through, about 7 minutes.

tortilla soup

why this recipe works Packed with layers of ingredients, this tortilla soup is a classic Mexican meal in a bowl full of authentic flavor yet is very easy to prepare. The classic recipe has three main components—the flavor base, the chicken stock, and the garnishes; we came up with a manageable approach to each. Typically, the vegetables for the flavor base are charred on a *comal* (griddle) and then pureed and fried. To simplify, we made a puree from smoky chipotles plus tomatoes, onion, garlic, and jalapeño, and fried the puree in oil over high heat. We poached chicken in store-bought broth infused with onion, garlic, cilantro, and oregano, which gave our base plenty of flavor without a from-scratch stock. We oven-toasted tortilla strips instead of frying them. For mild spiciness, trim the ribs and seeds from the jalapeño (or omit it altogether) and use 1 teaspoon chipotle chile pureed with the tomatoes in step 3. For a spicier soup, add up to 1 tablespoon adobo sauce in step 5 before you add the chicken. Although the chicken and broth can be prepared ahead of time, the tortilla strips and garnishes are best prepared the day of serving.

serves 8

8 (6-inch) corn tortillas, cut into ½-inch-wide strips

2 tablespoons vegetable oil

Salt

1½ pounds bone-in split chicken breasts, trimmed

8 cups chicken broth

1 large white onion, quartered

4 garlic cloves, peeled

8–10 sprigs fresh cilantro, plus leaves for serving

1 sprig fresh oregano

2 tomatoes, cored and quartered

½ jalapeño chile

1 tablespoon minced canned chipotle chile in adobo sauce

1 avocado, halved, pitted, and diced

8 ounces Cotija cheese, crumbled (2 cups)

Lime wedges

1. Adjust oven rack to middle position and heat oven to 425 degrees. Toss tortilla strips with 1 tablespoon oil and bake on rimmed baking sheet until crisp and deep golden, about 14 minutes, stirring occasionally. Season lightly with salt and let cool on paper towel–lined plate.

2. Meanwhile, bring chicken, broth, 2 onion quarters, 2 garlic cloves, cilantro sprigs, oregano sprig, and ½ teaspoon salt to boil over medium-high heat in Dutch oven. Reduce heat to low, cover, and simmer gently until chicken registers 160 degrees, about 20 minutes. Transfer chicken to cutting board, let cool slightly, and shred into bite-size pieces, discarding skin and bones. Strain broth through fine-mesh strainer.

3. Puree tomatoes, jalapeño, chipotle, remaining 2 onion quarters, and remaining 2 garlic cloves in food processor until smooth. Heat remaining 1 tablespoon oil in now-empty Dutch oven over high heat until shimmering. Add tomato-onion puree and ⅛ teaspoon salt and cook, stirring frequently, until mixture has darkened in color, about 10 minutes.

4. Stir in strained broth and bring to boil, then reduce heat to low and simmer gently until flavors have blended, 15 to 20 minutes.

5. Stir in shredded chicken and let heat through, about 2 minutes. Place portions of tortilla strips in bowls, ladle soup over top, and serve with avocado, Cotija, cilantro leaves, and lime wedges.

to make ahead
Prepare recipe through step 4. Shredded chicken and broth can be refrigerated in separate containers for up to 2 days; return broth to simmer before proceeding.

why this recipe works While the name may conjure up images of another era, this cream of chicken soup is so decidedly fresh and satisfying that it will earn a spot on your regular dinner rotation. After testing many existing recipes, we found that we preferred the texture of shredded white meat in our soup. And for a soup with a silky texture, a roux was the easiest and best thickening method while reducing a little sherry proved an easy path to enhanced depth. To make our soup substantial, we added potatoes and carrots, along with leeks for sweetness. We wanted rich chicken flavor and knew that the fond (the browned bits on the bottom of the pot) that searing creates would help get us there. But we couldn't leave the browned chicken in the pot the entire time because it would overcook. Then we got a crazy idea: Could we take the skin off of the chicken and brown it alone to create fond, and then leave it in through the cooking process to extract even more flavor? We gave it a try, using the skin from split breasts. Eying the chicken fat in the pot, we decided to use it to help build the roux. We left the skin in the pot, added butter, and sautéed the leeks in the tasty fats. Then we eventually added the breasts and simmered them until they registered 160 degrees. We pulled the meat out to rest but continued to simmer the skin in the broth. When the meat cooled, we shredded it, removed the skin from the pot, and stirred the cream and chicken into the soup.

serves 6

1½ **pounds bone-in split chicken breasts, skin removed and reserved, trimmed**

Salt and pepper

1 tablespoon water

1 pound leeks, white and light green parts only, halved lengthwise, sliced ¼ inch thick, and washed thoroughly (2½ cups)

2 tablespoons unsalted butter

½ **cup all-purpose flour**

⅓ **cup dry sherry**

8 cups chicken broth

12 ounces Yukon Gold potatoes, peeled and cut into ¾-inch pieces

3 carrots, peeled and cut into ½-inch pieces

3 sprigs fresh thyme

1 bay leaf

½ **cup heavy cream**

3 tablespoons minced fresh chives

1. Season chicken with salt and pepper. Place water and chicken skin in Dutch oven and cook over medium-low heat with lid slightly ajar until enough fat has rendered from skin to coat bottom of pot, about 7 minutes.

2. Uncover pot, increase heat to medium, and continue to cook until skin has browned, about 3 minutes, flipping skin halfway through cooking. Add leeks and butter and cook until leeks are just softened, about 3 minutes. Stir in flour and cook for 1 minute. Stir in sherry and cook until evaporated, about 1 minute.

3. Slowly whisk in broth until incorporated. Add potatoes, carrots, thyme sprigs, bay leaf, and chicken and bring to boil. Reduce heat to medium-low and simmer, uncovered, until chicken registers 160 degrees, 20 to 25 minutes.

4. Transfer chicken to plate and let cool for 20 minutes. While chicken cools, continue to simmer soup for 20 minutes. Using shallow spoon, skim grease and foam from surface of soup. Discard chicken bones and shred meat into 1-inch pieces. Discard chicken skin, thyme sprigs, and bay leaf. Off heat, stir in cream and chicken. Season with salt and pepper to taste. Sprinkle individual portions with chives and serve.

mexican-style chicken and chickpea soup

why this recipe works *Caldo tlalpeño* is a smoky, spicy soup laden with tender pieces of shredded chicken, meaty chickpeas, and savory bites of avocado in a broth rich with the smoky flavor and spice of chipotle chiles. While many traditional recipes call for soaking dried chipotle chiles, we were happily surprised to see that just as many use the canned alternative. This fast, convenient option packed a deep, smoky punch, so we turned our attention to replacing a tough-to-find Mexican herb called epazote. Tests showed that a mix of cilantro and oregano provided a good approximation. Although the herbs are traditionally steeped in the broth while cooking, we found that mincing and stirring them in just before serving provided a burst of freshness that the finished soup needed. We built our soup base by first browning bone-in, skin-on chicken breasts (a traditional cut for this soup), developing flavorful fond in the pan. After removing the browned breasts, we softened our aromatic ingredients in the rendered chicken fat before stirring in a bit of flour, which produced a rich, deeply flavored broth with great substance. Zucchini, added along with the chickpeas, provided a fresh if nontraditional counterpoint to the rich soup. We shredded the chicken and added it back to the soup just a few minutes before serving to ensure that the delicate meat wouldn't overcook and turn tough. Serve with lime wedges, diced avocado, and/or sliced radishes.

serves 6 to 8

1½ pounds bone-in split chicken breasts, trimmed

Salt and pepper

1 tablespoon vegetable oil

2 onions, chopped fine

2 carrots, peeled and sliced ½ inch thick

5 garlic cloves, minced

2 teaspoons minced canned chipotle chile in adobo sauce

1½ teaspoons minced fresh thyme or ½ teaspoon dried

2 tablespoons all-purpose flour

8 cups chicken broth

2 zucchini, cut into ½-inch pieces

1 (15-ounce) can chickpeas, rinsed

3 tablespoons minced fresh cilantro

1 teaspoon minced fresh oregano

1. Pat chicken dry with paper towels and season with salt and pepper. Heat oil in Dutch oven over medium-high heat until just smoking. Brown chicken lightly, 2 to 3 minutes per side; transfer to plate.

2. Add onions and carrots to fat left in pot and cook over medium heat until softened and lightly browned, 8 to 10 minutes. Stir in garlic, chipotle, and thyme and cook until fragrant, about 30 seconds. Stir in flour and cook for 1 minute. Slowly whisk in broth, scraping up any browned bits, and bring to simmer.

3. Return browned chicken and any accumulated juices to pot, reduce heat to low, cover, and simmer gently until chicken registers 160 degrees, 15 to 20 minutes.

4. Transfer chicken to cutting board and let cool slightly. Using 2 forks, shred chicken into bite-size pieces; discard skin and bones. Meanwhile, stir zucchini and chickpeas into soup and simmer until zucchini is just tender, 5 to 10 minutes.

5. Stir shredded chicken into soup and simmer until heated through, about 2 minutes. Off heat, stir in cilantro and oregano and season with salt and pepper to taste. Serve.

italian chicken soup with parmesan dumplings

why this recipe works This rustic Northern Italian specialty features tender dumplings deeply flavored with Parmesan and served in a light chicken broth. We modernized the classic recipe a bit, making it more hearty and a bit easier by adding flavor to store-bought broth using browned chicken thighs. Fennel, carrots, and escarole complement the shredded chicken and the flavorful dumplings. To ensure that the dumplings remain intact during cooking, roll them until the surfaces are smooth and no cracks remain.

serves 4 to 6

1½ pounds bone-in chicken thighs, trimmed

Salt and pepper

1 teaspoon vegetable oil

1 fennel bulb, 1 tablespoon fronds minced, stalks discarded, bulb halved, cored, and cut into ½-inch pieces

1 onion, chopped fine

2 carrots, peeled and cut into ¾-inch pieces

½ cup dry white wine

8 cups chicken broth

1 Parmesan cheese rind, plus 3 ounces Parmesan, shredded (1 cup)

2 slices hearty white sandwich bread, torn into 1-inch pieces

2 large egg whites

¼ teaspoon grated lemon zest

Pinch ground nutmeg

½ small head escarole (6 ounces), trimmed and cut into ½-inch pieces

1. Pat chicken dry with paper towels and season with salt and pepper. Heat oil in Dutch oven over medium high heat until just smoking. Add chicken, skin side down, and cook until well browned, 6 to 8 minutes. Transfer chicken to plate. Discard skin.

2. Drain off all but 1 teaspoon fat from pot and reserve 1 tablespoon fat for dumplings. Return pot to medium heat. Add fennel bulb, onion, carrots, and ½ teaspoon salt and cook, stirring occasionally, until vegetables soften and begin to brown, about 5 minutes. Add wine and cook, scraping up any browned bits, until almost dry, about 2 minutes. Return chicken to pot; add broth and Parmesan rind and bring to boil. Reduce heat to low, cover, and simmer until chicken is tender and registers 175 degrees, about 30 minutes. Transfer chicken to plate. Discard Parmesan rind. Cover broth and remove from heat. When cool enough to handle, use 2 forks to shred chicken into bite-size pieces. Discard bones.

3. While broth is simmering, adjust oven rack to middle position and heat oven to 350 degrees. Pulse bread in food processor until finely ground, 10 to 15 pulses. Measure out 1 cup bread crumbs and transfer to parchment paper–lined rimmed baking sheet (set aside remainder for another use). Toast until light brown, about 5 minutes. Transfer to medium bowl, reserving sheet and parchment, and let bread crumbs cool completely.

4. Pulse shredded Parmesan in now-empty food processor until finely ground, 10 to 15 pulses. Transfer Parmesan to bowl with cooled bread crumbs and add reserved 1 tablespoon fat, egg whites, lemon zest, ⅛ teaspoon pepper, and nutmeg. Mix until thoroughly combined. Refrigerate dough for 15 minutes.

5. Working with 1 teaspoon dough at a time, roll into smooth balls and place on parchment-lined sheet (you should have about 28 dumplings).

6. Return broth to simmer over medium-high heat. Add escarole and chicken and return to simmer. Add dumplings and cook, adjusting heat to maintain gentle simmer, until dumplings float to surface and are cooked through, 3 to 5 minutes. Stir in fennel fronds. Season with salt and pepper to taste, and serve.

to make ahead
Prepare recipe through step 5. Refrigerate cooled broth, shredded chicken, and dumplings separately for up to 24 hours. To serve, proceed with step 6 as directed.

why this recipe works With this recipe in your arsenal, you can enjoy the addictive flavors of Thai soup any time, not just when dining out. For an authentic-tasting Thai chicken soup without all the hard-to-find ingredients, we began by making a rich base with chicken broth and coconut milk. Thai curry paste from the supermarket was an easy substitution for the assortment of obscure ingredients like kaffir lime leaves, galangal, and bird chiles used in from-scratch recipes. Pungent fish sauce and tart lime juice contributed the salty and sour flavors. Although we prefer the deeper, richer flavor of regular coconut milk, light coconut milk can be substituted for one or both cans. The fresh lemon grass can be omitted, but the soup will lack some complexity; don't be tempted to use jarred or dried lemon grass, as both have characterless flavor. If you want a spicier soup, add more red curry paste to taste. To make the chicken easier to slice, freeze it for 15 minutes.

serves 6

1 teaspoon vegetable oil

3 stalks lemon grass, bottom 5 inches only, minced

3 large shallots, chopped coarse

8 sprigs fresh cilantro, chopped, plus whole leaves for serving

3 tablespoons fish sauce

4 cups chicken broth

2 (13.5-ounce) cans coconut milk

1 tablespoon sugar

8 ounces white mushrooms, trimmed and sliced thin

1 pound boneless, skinless chicken breasts, trimmed, halved lengthwise, and sliced 1/4 inch thick

3 tablespoons lime juice (2 limes), plus wedges for serving

2 teaspoons Thai red curry paste

2 fresh Thai, serrano, or jalapeño chiles, stemmed, seeded, and sliced thin

2 scallions, sliced thin on bias

1. Heat oil in large saucepan over medium heat until shimmering. Add lemon grass, shallots, chopped cilantro sprigs, and 1 tablespoon fish sauce and cook, stirring often, until just softened but not browned, 2 to 5 minutes.

2. Stir in broth and 1 can coconut milk and bring to simmer. Cover, reduce heat to gentle simmer, and cook until flavors have blended, about 10 minutes. Strain broth through fine-mesh strainer. (Broth can be refrigerated for up to 1 day.)

3. Return strained broth to clean saucepan, stir in remaining can coconut milk and sugar, and bring to simmer. Stir in mushrooms and cook until just tender, 2 to 3 minutes. Stir in chicken and cook until no longer pink, 1 to 3 minutes.

4. Remove soup from heat. Whisk lime juice, curry paste, and remaining 2 tablespoons fish sauce together in bowl to dissolve curry, then stir mixture into soup. Ladle into bowls and sprinkle with cilantro leaves, chiles, and scallions. Serve with lime wedges.

mulligatawny with chicken

why this recipe works This classic Anglo-Indian soup features a potently spiced and pureed base enriched with lentils and tender shredded chicken. Its flavor profile comes from curry and other spices and coconut, which adds a touch of sweetness. After experimenting with store-bought curry powders and finding that the flavor of the soup was falling flat, we decided to make our own, as do most Indian home cooks, using a blend of garam masala, cumin, coriander, and turmeric. To give the finished soup the right amount of body, we made a roux with our aromatics, added the broth, and gently poached the bone-in chicken breasts which we had browned. Setting aside the chicken to cool, we pureed our soup to a smooth consistency and then added the lentils. While the lentils cooked through, we shredded the chicken. A dollop of yogurt and a sprinkling of cilantro were the crowning touches on our richly spiced, velvety mulligatawny. French green lentils (*lentilles du Puy*) will also work well here; the cooking time will remain the same. See page 4 for more information on pureeing soup.

serves 6

1½ pounds bone-in split chicken breasts, trimmed

Salt and pepper

1 tablespoon vegetable oil

2 tablespoons unsalted butter

2½ teaspoons garam masala

1½ teaspoons ground cumin

1½ teaspoons ground coriander

1 teaspoon ground turmeric

2 onions, chopped fine

2 carrots, peeled and chopped

1 celery rib, chopped

½ cup sweetened shredded or flaked coconut

4 garlic cloves, minced

4 teaspoons grated fresh ginger

¼ cup all-purpose flour

1 teaspoon tomato paste

7 cups chicken broth

½ cup dried brown lentils, picked over and rinsed

2 tablespoons minced fresh cilantro

1 cup plain yogurt, for serving

1. Pat chicken dry with paper towels and season with salt and pepper. Heat oil in Dutch oven over medium-high heat until just smoking. Brown chicken lightly on both sides, about 5 minutes, then transfer to plate.

2. Melt butter in now-empty Dutch oven over medium heat. Stir in garam masala, cumin, coriander, and turmeric and cook until fragrant, about 30 seconds. Stir in onions, carrots, celery, and coconut and cook until softened, 5 to 7 minutes. Stir in garlic and ginger and cook until fragrant, about 30 seconds. Stir in flour and tomato paste and cook for 1 minute. Gradually whisk in broth, scraping up any browned bits and smoothing out any lumps, and bring to boil.

3. Add browned chicken, cover, and simmer gently until chicken registers 160 degrees, 15 to 20 minutes. Remove chicken from pot, let cool slightly, then shred meat into bite-size pieces, discarding skin and bones.

4. Working in batches, puree soup until smooth, return to clean pot, and simmer. Stir in lentils, cover, and simmer gently until lentils are tender, 35 to 45 minutes.

5. Stir in shredded chicken and let it heat through, about 2 minutes. Off heat, stir in cilantro and season with salt and pepper to taste. Dollop individual portions with yogurt before serving.

spicy moroccan-style lamb and lentil soup (harira)

why this recipe works **Harira** is a heavily spiced, intensely flavored Moroccan soup of lentils, tomatoes, chickpeas, and often chicken or lamb that is rich and soul-satisfying. For this version we created a soup worthy of its North African heritage using an inexpensive cut of lamb: shoulder chops. After searing pieces of lamb and setting them aside, we built the stock with onion, tomato, and a laundry list of spices and then simmered the lamb, lentils, and chickpeas in the oven for even cooking and a hands-off method. We shredded the lamb before stirring it back in, and the texture of this meat made us swoon. This version was balanced, warming, and near perfect, but tasters wanted just a little more zing. We chose to finish the soup by stirring in a healthy portion of superspicy harissa paste, which gave incredible spice, heat, and depth. You can substitute store-bought harissa, though spiciness can vary greatly by brand. French green lentils (*lentilles du Puy*) will also work well here; the cooking time will remain the same. If you can't find lamb shoulder chops, you can substitute an equal amount of lamb shoulder roast trimmed of all visible fat.

serves 8

harissa
5 tablespoons extra-virgin olive oil

1½ tablespoons paprika

4 garlic cloves, minced

2 teaspoons ground coriander

¾ teaspoon ground cumin

¼ teaspoon cayenne pepper

⅛ teaspoon salt

soup
1 pound lamb shoulder chops, trimmed of all visible fat and cut into 2-inch pieces

Salt and pepper

1 tablespoon extra-virgin olive oil

1 onion, chopped fine

1 teaspoon grated fresh ginger

1 teaspoon ground cumin

½ teaspoon paprika

¼ teaspoon ground cinnamon

¼ teaspoon cayenne pepper

Pinch saffron threads, crumbled

1 tablespoon all-purpose flour

10 cups chicken broth

1 cup dried brown lentils, picked over and rinsed

4 plum tomatoes (about 1 pound), cored and cut into ¾-inch pieces

1 (15-ounce) can chickpeas, rinsed

⅓ cup minced fresh cilantro

1. for the harissa Combine all ingredients in medium bowl; microwave on high until bubbling and fragrant, 15 to 30 seconds. Set aside to cool.

2. for the soup Adjust oven rack to lower-middle position and heat oven to 325 degrees. Season lamb with salt and pepper. Heat oil in Dutch oven over medium-high heat until just smoking. Brown lamb on all sides, about 8 minutes; transfer to plate. Pour off all but 2 tablespoons fat from pot.

3. Reduce heat to medium, add onion to fat left in pot and cook until softened, 5 to 7 minutes.

Stir in ginger, cumin, paprika, cinnamon, cayenne, saffron, and ¼ teaspoon pepper and cook until fragrant, about 30 seconds. Stir in flour and cook for 1 minute. Gradually whisk in broth, scraping up any browned bits and smoothing out any lumps. Return lamb and any accumulated juices to pot, bring to simmer, and cook for 10 minutes. Add lentils, cover, place pot in oven, and cook until fork slips easily in and out of lamb and lentils are tender, about 50 minutes.

4. Remove lamb from pot, let cool slightly, then using 2 forks, shred lamb into bite-size pieces, discarding pieces of fat. Meanwhile, stir in tomatoes and chickpeas and continue to simmer until flavors meld, about 10 minutes longer. Stir in shredded lamb and let it heat through, about 2 minutes. Stir in cilantro and ¼ cup harissa, and season with salt and pepper to taste. Serve, passing extra harissa separately.

beef barley soup with mushrooms and thyme

why this recipe works The star of our beef barley soup is a rich, intensely flavored beef stock. We were able to make a from-scratch stock in about 2½ hours thanks to a lot of browned beef (we preferred shank) and a few small bones. As a bonus, the shank meat turned soft and gelatinous, perfect for shredding and adding to the soup. Mushrooms complement beefy flavor, so we used them for an even meatier-tasting soup. Mulling over the choice of what barley to use, we settled on pearl barley because it is a quicker-cooking grain. Adding fresh thyme early on allowed its robust flavor to infuse the broth evenly while diced tomatoes added complexity and some acidity and helped balance the heartiness of the barley. Making a beef noodle soup variation turned out to be a cinch: We simply swapped hearty wide egg noodles for the barley and simmered them right in the broth. You will need the stock and 2 cups of cooked beef (either from the shank or from the chuck) from Rich Beef Stock (page 168) for this recipe.

serves 6

2 tablespoons vegetable oil

1 onion, chopped

2 carrots, peeled and chopped

12 ounces white mushrooms, trimmed and sliced thin

1 recipe Rich Beef Stock (page 168) plus 2 cups meat, shredded into bite-size pieces

½ cup canned diced tomatoes, drained

½ cup pearl barley

1½ teaspoons minced fresh thyme or ½ teaspoon dried

¼ cup minced fresh parsley

Salt and pepper

1. Heat 1 tablespoon oil in stockpot or Dutch oven over medium heat until shimmering. Add onion and carrots and cook until vegetables are almost soft, 3 to 4 minutes. Add remaining 1 tablespoon oil and mushrooms and cook until mushrooms soften and liquid evaporates, 4 to 5 minutes longer.

2. Add beef stock and meat, tomatoes, barley, and thyme. Bring to boil, then reduce heat to low; simmer until barley is just tender, 45 to 50 minutes. Stir in parsley, season with salt and pepper to taste, and serve.

variation

beef noodle soup with mushrooms and thyme
Omit barley. After adding beef stock and meat, tomatoes, and thyme, bring soup to simmer and cook until vegetables are tender, about 15 minutes. Then, stir in 2 cups wide egg noodles and simmer until noodles are tender, 5 to 8 minutes. Stir in parsley, season with salt and pepper to taste, and serve.

mexican beef and vegetable soup

why this recipe works Mexico's version of beef and vegetable soup, *caldo de res*, is rich with spices, tender chunks of meat, and vegetables like tomatoes, corn, and squash. This recipe captures the authentic flavors of this classic soup while eliminating the long cooking time required by most traditional recipes. Our first step in streamlining the recipe was to eliminate bone-in cuts and focus on quicker-cooking boneless cuts. In the end, a beef chuck-eye roast proved to be our cut of choice—it was flavorful, tender, and juicy. We browned the meat and then set it aside while we sautéed garlic and onion. We found that sautéing some oregano and cumin along with our aromatics helped to bring out their flavors. We then added the broth (a combination of beef broth and chicken broth gave us the best flavor), returned the beef to the pot, and simmered everything until the meat was tender. Next, we considered which vegetables to add. Most authentic recipes call for chayote, a gourd-like fruit similar to a summer squash that is often used in Mexican cooking. Unfortunately, it is difficult to find in many parts of the United States, and we found its mild flavor disappointing. Zucchini lent a similar texture and had much more flavor. Tomatoes and corn are another mainstay in the soup. We found that canned diced tomatoes provided a more reliable flavor than fresh, but fresh corn on the cob was preferred over frozen kernels. We also included carrots and red potatoes, which contributed an earthiness that enriched the overall flavor of the soup. To maintain the rustic feel of the soup, we cut the corn and potatoes into large pieces. With a host of complex flavors and contrasting textures, our soup was now much less work than the original, but still just as hearty and delicious. Serve with lime wedges and/or sliced radishes.

serves 6 to 8

1 pound boneless beef chuck-eye roast, trimmed and cut into 1-inch pieces

Salt and pepper

1 tablespoon vegetable oil

1 onion, chopped

5 garlic cloves, minced

1 tablespoon minced fresh oregano or 1 teaspoon dried

1/2 teaspoon ground cumin

4 cups beef broth

2 cups chicken broth

1 (14.5-ounce) can diced tomatoes, drained

2 bay leaves

2 carrots, peeled and cut into 1/2-inch pieces

10 ounces red potatoes, unpeeled, cut into 1-inch pieces

1 zucchini, cut into 1/2-inch pieces

2 ears corn, husks and silk removed, cut into 1-inch rounds

2 tablespoons minced fresh cilantro

1. Pat beef dry with paper towels and season with salt and pepper. Heat oil in Dutch oven over medium-high heat until just smoking. Brown beef on all sides, 5 to 7 minutes; transfer to bowl.

2. Add onion to fat left in pot and cook over medium heat until softened, about 5 minutes. Stir in garlic, oregano, and cumin and cook until fragrant, about 30 seconds. Stir in beef broth, chicken broth, tomatoes, and bay leaves, scraping up any browned bits, and bring to simmer. Stir in browned beef with any accumulated juices, reduce heat to low, cover, and simmer gently for 30 minutes.

3. Stir in carrots and potatoes and simmer, uncovered, until beef and vegetables are just tender, 20 to 25 minutes. Stir in zucchini and corn and simmer until corn is tender, 5 to 10 minutes.

4. Off heat, discard bay leaves. Stir in cilantro and season with salt and pepper to taste. Serve.

italian wedding soup

why this recipe works This superflavorful soup is a match made in heaven: meatballs and tender greens. Traditional versions require hours just to build the meaty *brodo* for which this soup is famous but we wanted a recipe that was less of a project but still complexly flavored. Since it takes time to make the meatballs, we streamlined our recipe by using store-bought broth. Cooking garlic and red pepper flakes in extra-virgin olive oil before adding the broth added flavor, and poaching our meatballs in the broth added even more while also saving time. For the meatballs, meatloaf mix provided well-rounded flavor, which we boosted with garlic, parsley, oregano, and some Parmesan cheese. Some recipes call for stirring chopped spinach or escarole into the soup just before serving but we found these greens too bland. Chopped kale was a better option, adding great flavor and texture. If meatloaf mix isn't available, substitute 1 pound of 85 percent lean ground beef. Serve with extra Parmesan cheese and a drizzle of extra-virgin olive oil. Tubettini or ditalini can be used in place of the orzo.

serves 6 to 8

meatballs

2 slices hearty white sandwich bread, torn into pieces

½ cup milk

1 large egg yolk

1 ounce Parmesan cheese, grated (½ cup)

3 tablespoons chopped fresh parsley

3 garlic cloves, minced

¾ teaspoon salt

½ teaspoon pepper

½ teaspoon dried oregano

1 pound meatloaf mix

soup

1 tablespoon extra-virgin olive oil

2 garlic cloves, minced

¼ teaspoon red pepper flakes

12 cups chicken broth

1 large head kale or Swiss chard, stemmed, leaves chopped

1 cup orzo

3 tablespoons chopped fresh parsley

Salt and pepper

1. for the meatballs Using potato masher, mash bread and milk in large bowl until smooth. Add egg yolk, Parmesan, parsley, garlic, salt, pepper, and oregano and mash to combine. Add meatloaf mix and knead by hand until well combined. Form mixture into 1-inch meatballs (you should have about 55 meatballs) and arrange on rimmed baking sheet. Cover with plastic wrap and refrigerate until firm, at least 30 minutes. (Meatballs can be made up to 24 hours in advance.)

2. for the soup Heat oil in Dutch oven over medium-high heat until shimmering. Cook garlic and pepper flakes until fragrant, about 30 seconds. Add broth and bring to boil. Stir in kale and simmer until softened, 10 to 15 minutes. Stir in meatballs and pasta, reduce heat to medium, and simmer until meatballs are cooked through and pasta is tender, about 10 minutes. Stir in parsley and salt and pepper to taste. Serve.

why this recipe works This hearty soup, popular in Eastern Europe and Russia, deserves a place on the American table. We think its marriage of tender chunks of beef brisket and crisp, tangy cabbage is a winner, not to mention the rich broth infused with aromatics. To keep things easy, we used a mixture of store-bought beef and chicken broths, which provided just the right balance of flavor. Combining fresh cabbage with sauerkraut—an unconventional approach to this classic beef and cabbage soup—lent an extra level of flavor, and did so in minimum time. If you can't find savoy cabbage at your supermarket, you can substitute regular green cabbage; however, it has a less delicate texture. We tested store-bought sauerkraut and found that krauts packaged in shelf-stable jars and cans were fresher and brighter tasting than refrigerated products.

serves 4 to 6

1 (1-pound) beef brisket, flat cut, trimmed and cut into ½-inch pieces

Salt and pepper

2 tablespoons vegetable oil

1 onion, chopped

3 garlic cloves, minced

4 cups beef broth

4 cups chicken broth

2 bay leaves

2 carrots, peeled and cut into ½-inch pieces

½ small head savoy cabbage, quartered, cored, and shredded into ¼-inch-thick pieces

½ cup sauerkraut, rinsed

2 tablespoons minced fresh dill

Sour cream

1. Pat beef dry with paper towels and season with salt and pepper. Heat 2 teaspoons oil in Dutch oven over medium-high heat until just smoking. Brown half of beef on all sides, 5 to 7 minutes. (Reduce heat if fond begins to burn.) Transfer browned beef to medium bowl. Repeat with 2 teaspoons oil and remaining beef; transfer to bowl.

2. Heat remaining 2 teaspoons oil in pot over medium heat until shimmering. Add onion and cook until softened, 5 to 7 minutes. Stir in garlic and cook until fragrant, about 30 seconds.

3. Stir in beef broth and chicken broth, scraping up any browned bits. Stir in bay leaves and browned meat with any accumulated juices. Bring to boil, then cover, reduce to gentle simmer, and cook for 30 minutes.

4. Stir in carrots, cabbage, and sauerkraut. Cover partially (leaving pot open about 1 inch) and simmer gently until beef and vegetables are tender, 30 to 40 minutes longer.

5. Off heat, discard bay leaves. Stir in dill, season with salt and pepper to taste, and serve, passing sour cream separately.

vietnamese beef pho

why this recipe works The biggest selling point of this famous soup is its killer broth—a beefy, fragrant, faintly sweet concoction produced by simmering beef bones and water, along with ginger, onions, cinnamon, and star anise, for hours. To create a streamlined broth worthy of this recipe, we needed to think outside the box. It turns out that ground meat releases its flavor into liquid remarkably fast. The grinding process breaks up muscle fibers so a single pound of ground beef can transform 3 quarts of packaged broth in just 45 minutes. We then built out the fragrant dimension of our beefy broth with onion, fresh ginger, fish sauce, and warm spices. To serve, the hot broth is ladled over tender rice noodles and wafer-thin slices of easy-to-find strip steak. Look for rice noodles that are about 1/8 inch wide; these are often labeled "small." Do not use Thai Kitchen Stir-Fry Rice Noodles because they are too thick and don't adequately soak up the broth.

serves 4 to 6

1 pound 85 percent lean ground beef

2 onions, quartered through root end

12 cups beef broth

1/4 cup fish sauce, plus extra for seasoning

1 (4-inch) piece ginger, peeled and sliced into thin rounds

1 cinnamon stick

2 tablespoons sugar, plus extra for seasoning

6 star anise pods

6 whole cloves

Salt

1 teaspoon black peppercorns

1 (1-pound) boneless strip steak, trimmed and halved

14–16 ounces (1/8-inch-wide) rice noodles

1/3 cup chopped fresh cilantro

3 scallions, sliced thin (optional)

Bean sprouts

Sprigs fresh Thai or Italian basil

Lime wedges

Hoisin sauce

Sriracha sauce

1. Break ground beef into rough 1-inch chunks and drop in Dutch oven. Add water to cover by 1 inch. Bring mixture to boil over high heat. Boil for 2 minutes, stirring once or twice. Drain ground beef in colander and rinse well under running water. Wash out pot and return ground beef to pot.

2. Place 6 onion quarters in pot with ground beef. Slice remaining 2 onion quarters as thin as possible and set aside for garnish. Add broth, 2 cups water, fish sauce, ginger, cinnamon, sugar, star anise, cloves, 2 teaspoons salt, and peppercorns to pot and bring to boil over high heat. Reduce heat to medium-low and simmer, partially covered, for 45 minutes.

3. Pour broth through colander set in large bowl. Discard solids. Strain broth through fine-mesh strainer lined with triple thickness of cheesecloth; add water as needed to equal 11 cups. Return broth to

pot and season with extra sugar and salt (broth should taste over-seasoned). Cover and keep warm over low heat.

4. While broth simmers, place steak on large plate and freeze until very firm, 35 to 45 minutes. Once firm, cut against grain into 1/8-inch-thick slices. Return steak to plate and refrigerate until needed.

5. Place noodles in large container and cover with hot tap water. Soak until noodles are pliable, 10 to 15 minutes; drain noodles. Meanwhile, bring 4 quarts water to boil in large pot. Add drained noodles and cook until almost tender, 30 to 60 seconds. Drain immediately and divide noodles among individual bowls.

6. Bring broth to rolling boil over high heat. Divide steak among individual bowls, shingling slices on top of noodles. Pile reserved onion slices on top of steak slices and sprinkle with cilantro and scallions, if using. Ladle hot broth into each bowl. Serve immediately, passing bean sprouts, basil sprigs, lime wedges, hoisin, Sriracha, and extra fish sauce separately.

ramen soup with pork

serves 4

why this recipe works In Japan, ramen soup is a serious endeavor, with ramen shops on almost every street corner where the noodles are served in a variety of broths. Our favorite is a rich, meaty broth made from long-simmered pork bones. This version of ramen is garnished with thinly sliced pieces of tender pork, scallions, and toasted sesame seeds. We set out to duplicate this hearty bowl of noodles and keep it accessible to the home cook without compromising on flavor. For the pork we turned to convenient boneless country-style pork ribs, choosing to grind up 1/2 pound of the meat to add depth to a doctored chicken broth. After browning the ground pork we sautéed it with onion, garlic, and ginger before adding the broth and letting it all simmer. A little red miso added savory depth to our strained broth and all that was left to do was stir in the reserved sliced pork, soy sauce, mirin, and sesame oil and ladle it over ramen-filled serving bowls. The result was a Japanese treat prepared with little work but lots of authentic flavor. To make processing and slicing the pork easier, freeze it for 20 minutes. Supermarket ramen packages work well here (discard the accompanying seasoning packet), but dried ramen noodles can also be found at Asian markets. If you can't find miso, you can omit it, but the soup will have a less complex flavor. Since the pork will toughen if it sits in the broth too long, it is important to serve the soup immediately.

broth
1½ pounds boneless country-style pork ribs, trimmed

1 tablespoon vegetable oil

1 onion, chopped

6 garlic cloves, peeled and smashed

1 (1-inch) piece ginger, peeled, sliced into 1/4-inch-thick rounds, and smashed

8 cups chicken broth

soup
4 (3-ounce) packages ramen noodles, seasoning packets discarded

Salt

3 tablespoons red miso

2 tablespoons soy sauce

1 tablespoon mirin

1/2 teaspoon toasted sesame oil

2 scallions, sliced thin on bias

1 tablespoon sesame seeds, toasted

1. for the broth Slice 8 ounces pork ribs crosswise into 1/8-inch-thick slices; cover and refrigerate until needed. Cut remaining 1 pound pork ribs into 1-inch chunks, then pulse in food processor until coarsely ground, about 10 pulses.

2. Heat oil in Dutch oven over medium heat until shimmering. Add ground pork and cook, breaking up meat with wooden spoon, until well browned, about 10 minutes. Reduce heat to medium, then stir in onion, garlic, and ginger and cook until softened, about 2 minutes. Stir in broth, cover partially, and bring to simmer. Cook until broth is flavorful, about 40 minutes. Strain broth through fine-mesh strainer, discarding solids. (Broth can be refrigerated for up to 24 hours.)

3. for the soup Bring 4 quarts water to boil in large pot. Add noodles and 1 tablespoon salt and cook, stirring often, until just tender, about 2 minutes. Drain noodles and portion into bowls.

4. Return strained broth to clean saucepan and bring to simmer over medium-high heat. Whisk 1/2 cup of hot broth into miso until dissolved and smooth, then whisk miso mixture into broth in saucepan. Stir in soy sauce, mirin, sesame oil, and sliced pork. Cover, remove saucepan from heat, and let sit until pork is cooked through, about 3 minutes (do not overcook). Season with salt to taste. Ladle soup over noodles, sprinkle with scallions and sesame seeds, and serve.

chowders

73 farmhouse chicken chowder
   with corn, poblano chile, and cilantro
74 new england clam chowder
77 manhattan clam chowder
   italian-style manhattan clam chowder
78 new england fish chowder
81 lobster and corn chowder
83 fresh corn chowder
84 celeriac, fennel, and apple chowder

farmhouse chicken chowder

why this recipe works This hearty, rustic chicken chowder hails from landlocked rural America where it makes use of locally available foods. To create the ultimate chowder, we first made a rich chicken broth, which also provided white meat for the soup. We built layers of flavor by rendering smoky bacon and cooking the aromatics in the fat and added flour as a thickener. Then the broth was added along with potatoes and a few other vegetables. Once everything was tender we stirred in heavy cream to add richness and added the shredded chicken. The flavor of this soup depends on homemade broth; do not substitute store-bought.

serves 8

broth
1 (3½- to 4-pound) chicken

1 tablespoon vegetable oil

1 onion, chopped

8 cups water

2 teaspoons salt

2 bay leaves

chowder
4 slices bacon, chopped

1 onion, chopped fine

3 garlic cloves, minced

1 teaspoon minced fresh thyme or ¼ teaspoon dried

⅓ cup all-purpose flour

2 pounds Yukon Gold potatoes, peeled and cut into ½-inch pieces

1 carrot, peeled and sliced ¼ inch thick

1 red bell pepper, stemmed, seeded, and cut into ½-inch pieces

1 cup heavy cream

2 tablespoons minced fresh parsley

Salt and pepper

1. for the broth Cut chicken into 7 pieces: 2 split breasts, 2 legs, 2 wings, and a backbone. Set breasts aside, and hack remaining chicken into 2-inch pieces with cleaver. Heat oil in large Dutch oven over medium-high heat until just smoking. Add chicken breasts and brown lightly, about 5 minutes; transfer to plate.

2. Add half of 2-inch chicken pieces to pot and brown lightly, about 5 minutes; transfer to large bowl. Repeat with remaining pieces. Add onion to fat left in pot and cook until softened, about 3 minutes. Return chicken pieces (not breasts) to pot, cover, and reduce heat to low. Cook, stirring occasionally, until chicken has released its juices, about 20 minutes.

3. Add reserved chicken breasts, water, salt, and bay leaves and bring to boil. Cover, reduce heat to gentle simmer, and cook, skimming as needed, until chicken breasts register 160 degrees, about 20 minutes. Remove chicken breasts from pot, let cool slightly, then shred meat into bite-size pieces, discarding skin and bones. Strain broth through fine-mesh strainer, let stand for 10 minutes, then remove fat from surface.

4. for the chowder Cook bacon in Dutch oven over medium heat until crisp and rendered, 5 to 7 minutes; transfer half of bacon to paper towel–lined plate.

Add onion to bacon left in pot and cook until softened, 5 to 7 minutes. Stir in garlic and thyme and cook until fragrant, about 30 seconds. Stir in flour and cook for 1 minute.

5. Gradually whisk in broth, scraping up any browned bits and smoothing out any lumps. Stir in potatoes and carrot and bring to boil. Reduce to gentle simmer and cook until vegetables are nearly tender, about 10 minutes. Stir in bell pepper and simmer until all vegetables are tender, 10 to 15 minutes.

6. Stir in cream and bring to simmer. Stir in shredded chicken and let it heat through, about 2 minutes. Off heat, stir in parsley and season with salt and pepper to taste. Sprinkle individual portions with reserved bacon before serving.

variation
farmhouse chicken chowder with corn, poblano chile, and cilantro
If desired, you can substitute 1 cup thawed frozen corn for the fresh corn.

Substitute 1 stemmed, seeded, and chopped poblano chile for bell pepper. Add 1 ear corn, husk and silk removed, kernels cut from cob, and chile with carrot in step 5. Substitute minced fresh cilantro for parsley.

new england clam chowder

why this recipe works This recipe is chock-full of clams and classic briny, creamy chowder flavor. Starting with the clams, we settled on medium-size littlenecks or cherrystones since they offered good value and taste. We steamed the clams open instead of shucking them, which was easier and yielded clam broth. We also found that a ratio of 2 cups of our homemade broth to 3 cups of bottled clam juice gave enough clam taste without being too salty. We chose Yukon Gold potatoes, as their moderate levels of starch and moisture blended seamlessly with this creamy chowder. Thickening the chowder with flour helped to stabilize it, as it can otherwise easily separate and curdle. Cream turned out to be essential, but our chowder needed only a minimal amount, which provided richness without overpowering the flavor of the clams. Finally, we chose bacon rather than salt pork, a traditional component of chowder, to enrich the flavor with a subtle smokiness. Serve with oyster crackers.

serves 6

3 cups water

6 pounds medium hard-shell clams, such as cherrystones, scrubbed

2 slices bacon, chopped fine

2 onions, chopped fine

2 celery ribs, chopped fine

1 teaspoon minced fresh thyme or ¼ teaspoon dried

⅓ cup all-purpose flour

3 (8-ounce) bottles clam juice

1½ pounds Yukon Gold potatoes, peeled and cut into ½-inch pieces

1 bay leaf

1 cup heavy cream

2 tablespoons minced fresh parsley

Salt and pepper

1. Bring water to boil in Dutch oven over medium-high heat. Add clams, cover, and cook for 5 minutes. Stir clams thoroughly and continue to cook, covered, until they begin to open, 2 to 7 minutes. As clams open, transfer them to large bowl and let cool slightly. Discard any unopened clams.

2. Measure out and reserve 2 cups clam steaming liquid, avoiding any gritty sediment that has settled on bottom of pot. Open clams with paring knife, holding clams over bowl to catch any juices. Using knife, sever muscle that attaches clam belly to shell and transfer meat to cutting board. Discard shells. Chop clams coarse; set aside.

3. Clean now-empty Dutch oven, add bacon, and cook over medium heat until crisp, 5 to 7 minutes. Stir in onions and celery and cook until vegetables are softened, 5 to 7 minutes. Stir in thyme and cook until fragrant, about 30 seconds. Stir in flour and cook for 1 minute.

4. Gradually whisk in bottled clam juice and reserved clam steaming liquid, scraping up any browned bits and smoothing out any lumps. Stir in potatoes and bay leaf and bring to boil. Reduce heat to gentle simmer and cook until potatoes are tender, 20 to 25 minutes.

5. Stir in cream and return to brief simmer. Off heat, discard bay leaf, stir in parsley, and season with salt and pepper to taste. Stir in chopped clams, cover, and let warm through, about 1 minute. Serve.

to make ahead
After cooking potatoes until tender in step 4, chopped clams and soup can be refrigerated in separate containers for up to 1 day. Return broth to simmer before proceeding with step 5.

manhattan clam chowder

why this recipe works Our Manhattan clam chowder is head and shoulders above most versions because it has a briny bivalve taste right up front. This soup has a reputation for being boring because it's usually more about the tomatoes than the clams. Our secret? We use lots more clams and homemade clam broth to balance the strong flavor of the tomatoes and other vegetables. Medium-size hard-shell clams provided both the flavor for the broth and the clam meat for the chowder. We opted for canned diced tomatoes to let the clams take center stage. Smashing some of the tender potatoes released more of their starch and helped thicken the broth. When reheating, do not boil the chowder or it will toughen the clams. Use a Dutch oven or stockpot that holds 6 quarts or more and has a tight-fitting lid for this recipe.

serves 8

4 cups water

8 pounds medium hard-shell clams, such as cherrystones, scrubbed

2 slices thick-cut bacon, cut into 1/4-inch pieces

1 large onion, chopped fine

1 small red bell pepper, stemmed, seeded, and chopped fine

1 carrot, peeled and chopped fine

1 celery rib, chopped fine

4 garlic cloves, minced

1 teaspoon dried oregano

1/2 cup dry white wine

1 1/4 pounds Yukon Gold potatoes, peeled and cut into 1/4-inch pieces

1 (8-ounce) bottle clam juice

1 large bay leaf

2 (14.5-ounce) cans diced tomatoes

Salt and pepper

2 tablespoons chopped fresh parsley

1. Bring water to boil in Dutch oven over medium-high heat. Add clams, cover, and cook for 5 minutes. Stir clams thoroughly and continue to cook, covered, until they begin to open, 2 to 7 minutes. As clams open, transfer them to large bowl and let cool slightly. Discard any unopened clams. Measure out and reserve 5 cups clam steaming liquid, avoiding any gritty sediment that has settled on bottom of pot. (If broth measures less than 5 cups, add enough water to equal 5 cups.) Open clams with paring knife, holding clams over bowl to catch any juices. Using knife, sever muscle that attaches clam belly to shell and transfer meat to cutting board. Discard shells. Cut clams into 1/2-inch pieces; set aside.

2. Clean now-empty Dutch oven, add bacon, and cook over medium heat until crisp, 5 to 7 minutes. Add onion, bell pepper, carrot, and celery. Reduce heat to low, cover, and cook until softened, about 10 minutes. Add garlic and oregano and sauté until fragrant, about 1 minute.

3. Add wine and increase heat to high. Boil wine until it reduces by half, 2 to 3 minutes. Add potatoes, clam juice, bay leaf, and reserved clam broth. Bring to boil, reduce heat to medium-low, and simmer until potatoes are almost tender, 8 to 10 minutes. Using wooden spoon, smash a few potatoes against side of pot. Simmer to release potato starch, about 2 minutes.

4. Add tomatoes and their juice, return to simmer, and cook for 5 minutes. Off heat, stir in reserved clams and season with salt and pepper to taste; discard bay leaf. Stir in parsley and serve.

variation

italian-style manhattan clam chowder
Substitute 2 ounces finely chopped pancetta for bacon, increase garlic to 6 cloves, and add 1 teaspoon fennel seeds and 1/2 teaspoon red pepper flakes with garlic and oregano in step 2.

to make ahead
Prepare recipe up through discarding bay leaf in step 4 and refrigerate for up to 2 days. To reheat, warm over low heat until hot then stir in parsley just before serving.

new england fish chowder

serves 6 to 8

why this recipe works This modern fish chowder honors its simple roots by showcasing moist, tender morsels of fish in a delicate broth. Searching for a route to fresher, cleaner flavors, we got a bonus: shorter cooking time. We started by gently poaching meaty cod in water flavored with salt pork, onions, and herbs, which created a quick fish stock and eliminated any chance of over-cooking the fish. We added whole milk to this stock, as opposed to other rich dairy like half-and-half and heavy cream, to keep the chowder light and fresh-tasting and preserve the flavor of the cod. A tablespoon of cornstarch whisked into the milk before adding it to the pot coated its proteins, preventing it from curdling as the soup simmered. To keep the salt pork flavor from becoming overbearing, we left it in two large chunks that didn't produce as much browning and used butter to sweat the onions. Haddock, or other flaky white fish, may be substituted for the cod. Garnish the chowder with minced fresh chives, crisp bacon bits, or oyster crackers.

2 tablespoons unsalted butter

2 onions, cut into ½-inch dice

4 ounces salt pork, rind removed, rinsed, and cut into 2 pieces

1½ teaspoons minced fresh thyme

Salt and pepper

1 bay leaf

5 cups water

2 pounds skinless cod fillets, sliced crosswise into 6 equal pieces

1½ pounds Yukon Gold potatoes, peeled and cut into ½-inch dice

2 cups whole milk

1 tablespoon cornstarch

1. Melt butter in Dutch oven over medium heat. Add onions, salt pork, thyme, ¾ teaspoon salt, and bay leaf; cook, stirring occasionally, until onions are softened but not browned, 3 to 5 minutes. Add water and bring to simmer. Remove pot from heat, gently place cod fillets in water, cover, and let fish stand until opaque and nearly cooked through, about 5 minutes. Using metal spatula, transfer cod to bowl.

2. Return pot to medium-high heat, add potatoes, and bring to simmer. Cook until potatoes are tender and beginning to break apart, about 20 minutes.

3. Meanwhile, whisk milk, cornstarch, and ½ teaspoon pepper together in bowl. Stir milk mixture into chowder and return to simmer. Return fish and any accumulated juices to pot. Remove pot from heat, cover, and let stand for 5 minutes. Discard salt pork and bay leaf. Stir gently with wooden spoon to break fish into large pieces. Season with salt and pepper to taste. Serve immediately.

lobster and corn chowder

why this recipe works The combination of succulent lobster and sweet summer corn is hard to resist and this luxurious chowder is perhaps our favorite way to enjoy this pairing. For big lobster flavor, we made a lobster broth using the bodies. Sautéing them until they were bright red and lightly browned created better flavor, and adding a classic *mirepoix* of onion, carrot, and celery and white wine made a potent broth that we later used to poach the rest of the lobster. Bacon provided the chowder with a meaty backbone, while a bit of flour gave it body. For a fresh finish, we added a splash of dry sherry and parsley. Do not be tempted to substitute frozen corn for the fresh corn here; fresh corn is crucial to the flavor of this soup.

serves 4 to 6

broth
2 (1- to 1¼-pound) live lobsters

3 tablespoons vegetable oil

1 onion, chopped

1 carrot, peeled and chopped

1 celery rib, chopped

2 plum tomatoes, cored and cut into ½-inch pieces

⅓ cup dry white wine

7 cups water

1 bay leaf

chowder
2 ounces (about 2 slices) bacon, chopped fine

1 onion, chopped fine

1 celery rib, chopped fine

1 teaspoon minced fresh thyme or ¼ teaspoon dried

¼ cup all-purpose flour

1 large Yukon Gold potato (10 to 12 ounces), peeled and cut into ½-inch pieces

2 ears corn, husk and silk removed, kernels cut off cobs, and cobs scraped clean of pulp

¾ cup heavy cream

2 tablespoons minced fresh parsley

2 teaspoons dry sherry

Salt and pepper

1. for the broth Freeze lobsters for 5 to 10 minutes to sedate them (do not overfreeze). Holding each lobster firmly with dish towel, plunge tip of heavy-duty chef's knife into body at point where shell forms "T" to kill lobster. Move blade straight down through head to sever. Rotate lobster in opposite direction and, while holding upper body with one hand, cut through body toward tail to split in half lengthwise. Using spoon and fingers, discard innards (brain sac, green colored tomalley, and roe) and feathery gills. Using your hands, twist claws (with arms) and tail free from body; discard rubber bands.

2. Heat oil in large Dutch oven over medium-high heat until just smoking. Add cleaned lobster bodies and cook until bright red and lightly browned, 3 to 5 minutes. Stir in onion, carrot, celery, and tomatoes and cook until vegetables are softened, 5 to 7 minutes. Stir in wine and cook until nearly evaporated, about 1 minute.

3. Stir in water and bay leaf and bring to boil. Add lobster claws and tails, reduce to gentle simmer, and cook for 4 minutes. Remove claws and tails from pot and let cool slightly. Remove lobster meat from shells, cut into ½-inch pieces, and refrigerate until needed.

4. Meanwhile, continue to simmer lobster broth until rich and flavorful, about 45 minutes. Strain broth through a fine-mesh strainer, pressing on solids to release as much liquid as possible.

5. for the chowder Cook bacon in large Dutch oven over medium heat until rendered and crisp, 5 to 7 minutes. Stir in onion and celery and cook until vegetables are softened, 5 to 7 minutes. Stir in thyme and cook until fragrant, about 30 seconds. Stir in flour and cook for 1 minute.

6. Gradually whisk in strained lobster broth, scraping up any browned bits and smoothing out any lumps. Stir in potato and corn cob pulp and bring to boil. Reduce to gentle simmer and cook until potato is nearly tender, 15 to 20 minutes.

7. Stir in corn kernels and continue to simmer until tender, 5 to 7 minutes. Stir in cream and bring to a brief simmer. Off heat, remove bay leaf, stir in parsley and sherry, and season with salt and pepper to taste. Stir in lobster meat, cover, and let stand until warmed through, about 1 minute. Serve.

fresh corn chowder

why this recipe works This thick and lush chowder is bursting with fresh corn flavor. Contributing to that flavor was bacon; we used the rendered fat to sauté onion and garlic and create a richly flavored base. We learned that water diluted the flavor of the chowder so we used chicken broth as our liquid. To pump up the corn flavor, we first added grated corn and corn milk, which came from scraping the cobs with the back of a butter knife, then we stirred in more whole kernels toward the end. With whole milk as our primary dairy component (we rejected all heavy cream as too rich), we added a few tablespoons of flour, which thickened our soup nicely. This soup tastes best with sweet corn from the height of the season; do not substitute frozen corn.

serves 6

10 ears corn, husks and silk removed

4 slices bacon, chopped fine

1 onion, chopped fine

2 garlic cloves, minced

3 tablespoons all-purpose flour

3 cups chicken broth

2 cups whole milk

12 ounces red potatoes, unpeeled and cut into 1/4-inch cubes

2 bay leaves

1 teaspoon minced fresh thyme or 1/4 teaspoon dried

1 cup heavy cream

2 tablespoons minced fresh parsley

Salt and pepper

1. Working with 1 ear of corn at a time, stand 4 ears on end inside large bowl and cut kernels from cob using paring knife. Grate remaining 6 ears over large holes of box grater into separate bowl. Using back of butter knife, scrape remaining pulp from all cobs into bowl with grated corn.

2. Cook bacon in Dutch oven over medium heat until crisp, 5 to 7 minutes. Stir in onion and cook until softened, 5 to 7 minutes. Stir in garlic and cook until fragrant, about 30 seconds. Stir in flour and cook for 1 minute. Slowly stir in broth and milk, scraping up any browned bits. Stir in potatoes, bay leaves, thyme, and grated corn and pulp mixture. Bring to simmer and cook until potatoes are almost tender, about 15 minutes.

3. Stir in remaining corn kernels and cream. Continue to simmer until corn kernels are tender yet still slightly crunchy, about 5 minutes. Discard bay leaves. Stir in parsley and season with salt and pepper to taste. Serve.

celeriac, fennel, and apple chowder

why this recipe works This inspired sweet-and-savory vegetarian chowder combines hearty potato with delicately anise-flavored celery root and shredded apple. Celeriac (known more commonly as celery root) is a staple in supermarkets, but most cooks walk right by it. That's a shame because this knobby tuber boasts refreshing herbal flavors with notes of anise, mint, mild radish, and celery. Its creamy (rather than starchy) texture makes it the perfect choice for a hearty vegetable chowder. To further enhance its anise flavor, we sautéed a chopped fennel bulb along with pieces of onion. For a sweet, fruity counterpoint, we added some grated apple along with chunks of tender red potatoes to bulk up the chowder. For a bright citrus note, we simmered a strip of orange zest in the broth. Pureeing 2 cups of the chowder with a modest amount of cream and then stirring the puree back into the pot gave our soup the perfect amount of body. Finally, we stirred in minced fresh fennel fronds to brighten the dish.

serves 6

2 tablespoons unsalted butter

1 onion, cut into ½-inch pieces

1 fennel bulb, 1 tablespoon fronds minced, stalks discarded, bulb halved, cored, and cut into ½-inch pieces

Salt and pepper

6 garlic cloves, minced

2 teaspoons minced fresh thyme or ¾ teaspoon dried

2 tablespoons all-purpose flour

½ cup dry white wine

4 cups vegetable broth

1½ cups water

1 celery root (14 ounces), peeled and cut into ½-inch pieces

12 ounces red potatoes, unpeeled, cut into ½-inch pieces

1 Golden Delicious apple, peeled and shredded

1 bay leaf

1 (3-inch) strip orange zest

¼ cup heavy cream

1. Melt butter in Dutch oven over medium heat. Add onion, fennel bulb, and 1½ teaspoons salt and cook until vegetables are softened, 5 to 7 minutes. Stir in garlic and thyme and cook until fragrant, about 30 seconds. Stir in flour and cook for 1 minute. Stir in wine, scraping up any browned bits, and cook until nearly evaporated, about 1 minute.

2. Stir in broth, water, celery root, potatoes, apple, bay leaf, and orange zest and bring to boil. Reduce heat to low, partially cover, and simmer gently until stew is thickened and vegetables are tender, 35 to 40 minutes.

3. Off heat, discard bay leaf and orange zest. Puree 2 cups chowder and cream in blender until smooth, about 1 minute, then return to pot. Stir in fennel fronds, season with salt and pepper to taste, and serve.

modern
vegetable
soups

88 super greens soup with lemon-tarragon cream
90 provençal vegetable soup (soupe au pistou)
93 farmhouse vegetable and barley soup
94 wild rice and mushroom soup
97 country-style potato-leek soup
    with kielbasa
    with white beans
99 hearty cabbage soup
100 artichoke soup à la barigoule
102 beet and wheat berry soup with dill cream
105 vegetable shabu-shabu with sesame sauce
106 ultimate french onion soup
109 garlic-potato soup
110 classic gazpacho
    spicy gazpacho with chipotle chile and lime

super greens soup with lemon-tarragon cream

why this recipe works This deceptively delicious, silky-smooth soup delivers a big dose of healthy greens and boasts a deep, complex flavor brightened with a garnish of lemon and herb cream. First, we built a flavorful foundation of sweet caramelized onions and earthy sautéed mushrooms. We added broth, water, and lots of leafy greens (we liked a mix of chard, kale, arugula, and parsley), and simmered the greens until tender before blending them until smooth. We were happy with the soup's depth of flavor, but it was watery and too thin. Many recipes we found used potatoes as a thickener, but they lent an overwhelmingly earthy flavor. Instead, we tried using Arborio rice. The rice's high starch content thickened the soup to a velvety, lush consistency without clouding the vegetables' bright flavors. For a vibrant finish, we whisked together heavy cream, sour cream, lemon zest, lemon juice, and tarragon and drizzled it over the top.

serves 4 to 6

¼ cup heavy cream

3 tablespoons sour cream

2 tablespoons plus ½ teaspoon extra-virgin olive oil

¼ teaspoon finely grated lemon zest plus ½ teaspoon juice

½ teaspoon minced fresh tarragon

Salt and pepper

1 onion, halved through root end and sliced thin

¾ teaspoon light brown sugar

3 ounces white mushrooms, trimmed and sliced thin

2 garlic cloves, minced

Pinch cayenne pepper

3 cups water

3 cups vegetable broth

⅓ cup Arborio rice

12 ounces Swiss chard, stemmed and chopped coarse

9 ounces kale, stemmed and chopped coarse

¼ cup fresh parsley leaves

2 ounces (2 cups) baby arugula

1. Combine cream, sour cream, ½ teaspoon oil, lemon zest and juice, tarragon, and ¼ teaspoon salt in bowl. Cover and refrigerate until ready to serve.

2. Heat remaining 2 tablespoons oil in Dutch oven over medium-high heat. Stir in onion, sugar, and 1 teaspoon salt and cook, stirring occasionally, until onion releases some moisture, about 5 minutes. Reduce heat to low and cook, stirring often and scraping up any browned bits, until onion is deeply browned and slightly sticky, about 30 minutes. (If onion is sizzling or scorching, reduce heat. If onion is not browning after 15 to 20 minutes, increase heat.)

3. Stir in mushrooms and cook until they have released their moisture, about 5 minutes. Stir in garlic and cayenne and cook until fragrant, about 30 seconds. Stir in water, broth, and rice, scraping up any browned bits, and bring to boil. Reduce heat to low, cover, and simmer for 15 minutes.

4. Stir in chard, kale, and parsley, 1 handful at a time, until wilted and submerged in liquid. Return to simmer, cover, and cook until greens are tender, about 10 minutes.

5. Off heat, stir in arugula until wilted. Working in batches, process soup in blender until smooth, about 1 minute. Return pureed soup to clean pot and season with salt and pepper to taste. Drizzle individual portions with lemon-tarragon cream and serve.

provençal vegetable soup
(soupe au pistou)

why this recipe works This is a great soup to make in the summer when farmers' markets are overflowing with green beans, zucchini, and bunches of fresh basil. It is a classic summer soup with a delicate broth that is intensified by a dollop of pistou, the French equivalent of Italy's pesto. Leeks, green beans, and zucchini all made the cut for this recipe; we liked their summery flavors, different shapes, and varying shades of green. We added canned white beans (which were far more convenient than dried in this quick-cooking soup) and orecchiette pasta (for its easy-to-spoon shape). To simplify the traditional pistou, we just whirred basil, Parmesan, olive oil, and garlic together in our food processor. If you cannot find haricots verts (thin green beans), substitute regular green beans and cook them for an extra minute or two. You can substitute small shells or ditalini for the orecchiette (the cooking times might vary slightly). We prefer broth prepared from our Vegetable Broth Base (page 174), but store-bought vegetable broth can be used. Serve with Garlic Toasts (page 11) or crusty bread, if desired.

serves 6

pistou
3/4 cup fresh basil leaves

1 ounce Parmesan cheese, grated (1/2 cup)

1/3 cup extra-virgin olive oil

1 garlic clove, minced

soup
1 tablespoon extra-virgin olive oil

1 leek, white and light green parts only, halved lengthwise, sliced 1/2 inch thick, and washed thoroughly

1 celery rib, cut into 1/2-inch pieces

1 carrot, peeled and sliced 1/4 inch thick

Salt and pepper

2 garlic cloves, minced

3 cups vegetable broth

3 cups water

1/2 cup orecchiette or other short pasta

8 ounces haricots verts or green beans, trimmed and cut into 1/2-inch lengths

1 (15-ounce) can cannellini or navy beans

1 small zucchini, halved lengthwise, seeded, and cut into 1/4-inch pieces

1 large tomato, cored, seeded, and cut into 1/4-inch pieces

1. for the pistou Process all ingredients in food processor until smooth, scraping down sides of bowl as needed, about 15 seconds. (Pistou can be refrigerated for up to 4 hours.)

2. for the soup Heat oil in large Dutch oven over medium heat until shimmering. Add leek, celery, carrot, and 1/2 teaspoon salt and cook until vegetables are softened, 8 to 10 minutes. Stir in garlic and cook until fragrant, about 30 seconds. Stir in broth and water and bring to simmer.

3. Stir in pasta and simmer until slightly softened, about 5 minutes. Stir in haricots verts and simmer until bright green but still crunchy, 3 to 5 minutes. Stir in cannellini beans and their liquid, zucchini, and tomato and simmer until pasta and vegetables are tender, about 3 minutes. Season with salt and pepper to taste. Top individual portions with generous tablespoon pistou and serve.

why this recipe works This simple, satisfying soup features lots of vegetables accented by nutty, chewy grains of barley. We started by simmering leeks, carrots, and celery in a combination of wine and soy sauce until we had a potent aromatic backbone for our soup. Then we added the barley along with broth, dried porcini mushrooms, and herbs. As the barley softened, the mushrooms and herbs infused the broth with flavor. Next, we added the remaining vegetables: chunks of Yukon Gold potatoes, turnip, and some cabbage. Once all the vegetables were tender, we stirred in some frozen peas, lemon juice, and parsley for a pop of bright flavor. We prefer an acidic, unoaked white wine such as Sauvignon Blanc for this recipe. Garnish this soup with crumbled cheddar cheese or Herbed Croutons (page 11).

serves 6 to 8

8 sprigs fresh parsley plus 3 tablespoons chopped

4 sprigs fresh thyme

1 bay leaf

2 tablespoons unsalted butter or vegetable oil

1½ pounds leeks, white and light green parts only, halved lengthwise, sliced ½ inch thick, and washed thoroughly

2 carrots, peeled and cut into ½-inch pieces

2 celery ribs, cut into ¼-inch pieces

⅓ cup dry white wine

2 teaspoons soy sauce

Salt and pepper

6 cups water

4 cups chicken broth or vegetable broth

½ cup pearl barley

1 garlic clove, peeled and smashed

⅛ ounce dried porcini mushrooms, finely ground using spice grinder

1½ pounds Yukon Gold potatoes, peeled and cut into ½-inch pieces

8 ounces turnip, peeled and cut into ¾-inch pieces

1½ cups chopped green cabbage

1 cup frozen peas

1 teaspoon lemon juice

1. Using kitchen twine, tie together parsley sprigs, thyme sprigs, and bay leaf. Melt butter in Dutch oven over medium heat. Add leeks, carrots, celery, wine, soy sauce, and 2 teaspoons salt. Cook, stirring occasionally, until liquid has evaporated and celery is softened, about 10 minutes.

2. Stir in water, broth, barley, garlic, mushroom powder, and herb bundle. Increase heat to high and bring to boil. Reduce heat to medium-low, partially cover, and simmer gently for 25 minutes.

3. Stir in potatoes, turnip, and cabbage and simmer until barley, potatoes, turnip, and cabbage are tender, 18 to 20 minutes. Off heat, discard herb bundle. Stir in peas, lemon juice, and chopped parsley. Season with salt and pepper to taste, and serve.

wild rice and mushroom soup

why this recipe works Earthy, creamy, and bursting with mushroom flavor, this soup belies the simplicity of its humble ingredients. We kept the focus on the rice and mushrooms by choosing supporting players that amplified the nutty, umami-rich flavor profile we were after: tomato paste, soy sauce, dry sherry, and plenty of garlic. For the mushrooms, we chose fresh cremini mushrooms and added dried shiitakes for a dose of potent mushroom flavor. Grinding the shiitakes ensured that their flavor permeated the broth. Simmering the wild rice with baking soda decreased its cooking time and brought out more robust flavor. We used the rice simmering liquid as part of our broth, infusing the entire soup with wild rice flavor. Cornstarch helped thicken the broth, and some cream gave our soup a velvety texture. We finished the soup with chives and lemon zest for brightness. White mushrooms can be substituted for the cremini mushrooms. We used a spice grinder to process the dried shiitake mushrooms, but a blender also works.

serves 6 to 8

4¼ cups water

1 sprig fresh thyme

1 bay leaf

5 garlic cloves, peeled (1 whole, 4 minced)

Salt and pepper

¼ teaspoon baking soda

1 cup wild rice

4 tablespoons unsalted butter

1 pound cremini mushrooms, trimmed and sliced ¼ inch thick

1 onion, chopped fine

1 teaspoon tomato paste

⅔ cup dry sherry

¼ ounce dried shiitake mushrooms, finely ground using spice grinder

4 cups chicken or vegetable broth

1 tablespoon soy sauce

¼ cup cornstarch

½ cup heavy cream

¼ cup minced fresh chives

¼ teaspoon finely grated lemon zest

1. Adjust oven rack to middle position and heat oven to 375 degrees. Bring 4 cups water, thyme sprig, bay leaf, whole garlic clove, ¾ teaspoon salt, and baking soda to boil in medium saucepan over high heat. Add rice and return to boil. Cover saucepan, transfer to oven, and bake until rice is tender, 35 to 50 minutes. Drain rice in fine-mesh strainer set in 4-cup liquid measuring cup, discarding thyme sprig, bay leaf, and garlic. Add enough water to reserved cooking liquid to measure 3 cups.

2. Melt butter in Dutch oven over high heat. Add cremini, onion, tomato paste, minced garlic, ¾ teaspoon salt, and 1 teaspoon pepper. Cook, stirring occasionally, until vegetables are browned and dark fond develops on bottom of pot, about 15 minutes.

3. Stir in sherry, scraping up any browned bits, and cook until nearly evaporated, about 2 minutes. Stir in ground shiitakes, broth, soy sauce, and reserved rice cooking liquid and bring to boil. Reduce heat to low, cover, and simmer until onion and mushrooms are tender, about 20 minutes.

4. Whisk cornstarch and remaining ¼ cup water together in bowl. Stir cornstarch slurry into soup and simmer until thickened, about 2 minutes. Off heat, stir in cooked rice, cream, chives, and lemon zest. Cover and let stand for 20 minutes. Season with salt and pepper to taste, and serve.

country-style potato-leek soup

why this recipe works This is the ultimate potato-leek soup: It's hearty with just the right proportion of leeks to potatoes. As an added bonus, it's quick and easy to prepare and you can easily vary it by adding kielbasa or white beans. We found that low-starch red potatoes were the best option for a flavorful country-style potato-leek soup because they held their shape and didn't become waterlogged during cooking. In addition, we removed the pot from the heat toward the end to allow the potatoes to finish cooking in the hot broth without becoming overcooked or mushy. Sautéing plenty of leeks in butter helped pump up the flavor, and leaving our soup full of chunks of potato and pieces of leek kept up the rustic theme. Leeks can vary in size. If yours have large white and light green sections, use fewer leeks.

serves 6 to 8

6 tablespoons unsalted butter

4–5 pounds leeks, white and light green parts only, halved lengthwise, sliced 1 inch thick, and washed thoroughly (11 cups)

1 tablespoon all-purpose flour

5¼ cups chicken broth

1 bay leaf

1¾ pounds red potatoes, peeled and cut into ¾-inch chunks

Salt and pepper

1. Melt butter in Dutch oven over medium heat. Stir in leeks, cover, and cook, stirring occasionally, until leeks are tender but not mushy, 15 to 20 minutes (do not brown). Stir in flour and cook for 2 minutes.

2. Increase heat to high and gradually stir in broth. Stir in bay leaf and potatoes, cover, and bring to boil. Reduce heat to medium-low and simmer, covered, until potatoes are almost tender, 5 to 7 minutes.

3. Remove from heat and let stand until potatoes are tender and flavors meld, 10 to 15 minutes. Discard bay leaf and season with salt and pepper to taste. Serve. (Soup can be refrigerated for up to 2 days; add water as needed when reheating to adjust consistency.)

variations

country-style potato-leek soup with kielbasa

Eight ounces of cooked ham, cut into ½-inch dice, can be substituted for the sausage, if desired. Whichever you choose, season the soup with care, since both ham and kielbasa are fully seasoned.

Before removing pot from heat, stir in 8 ounces kielbasa sausage, cut into ½-inch slices.

country-style potato-leek soup with white beans

Reduce potatoes to 12 ounces. Before removing pot from heat, stir in 1 cup hot water and 1 cup canned cannellini beans.

hearty cabbage soup

why this recipe works The combination of assertive aromatics and fresh herbs gives cabbage and potatoes an unexpected star quality in this satisfying soup. We started our testing with the cabbage. Tasters preferred the stronger flavor of green cabbage over napa or savoy cabbage. For the potatoes, low-starch red potatoes beat out other varieties because they held their shape after a period of simmering. Many cabbage soup recipes also call for a pork product—most often smoky bacon. We swapped out the bacon for hot smoked paprika. This gave the soup more backbone and a hint of smokiness. We also added caraway seeds for their delicate anise flavor, which brought out the sweetness of the cabbage, and we finished the soup with fresh dill. A dollop of sour cream added a rich, tangy counterpoint to the sweetness of the soup. You can substitute smoked paprika and a pinch of cayenne for the hot smoked paprika.

serves 6 to 8

3 tablespoons unsalted butter

1 onion, chopped fine

Salt and pepper

4 garlic cloves, minced

1 teaspoon caraway seeds

1 teaspoon minced fresh thyme or ¼ teaspoon dried

½ teaspoon hot smoked paprika

¼ cup dry white wine

6 cups vegetable broth

1 small head green cabbage (1¼ pounds), cored and cut into ¾-inch pieces

12 ounces red potatoes, unpeeled and cut into ¾-inch pieces

3 carrots, peeled and cut into ½-inch pieces

1 bay leaf

1 tablespoon minced fresh dill

1 cup sour cream

1. Melt butter in Dutch oven over medium heat. Stir in onion and 1 teaspoon salt and cook until softened, 5 to 7 minutes. Stir in garlic, caraway, thyme, and paprika and cook until fragrant, about 30 seconds.

2. Stir in wine, scraping up any browned bits, and simmer until nearly evaporated, about 1 minute. Stir in broth, cabbage, potatoes, carrots, and bay leaf and bring to boil. Cover, reduce to gentle simmer, and cook until vegetables are tender, about 30 minutes.

3. Discard bay leaf. Season with salt and pepper to taste, and sprinkle with dill. Top individual portions with sour cream and serve.

artichoke soup à la barigoule

why this recipe works Barigoule is a traditional Provençal dish of braised artichokes, mushrooms, and root vegetables. We thought the combination of delicate yet earthy artichokes and meaty mushrooms would translate well into a satisfying soup. To amplify their flavors, we worked to enhance each of the core components. We started by searing artichokes to intensify their subtle flavor. Cooking the mushrooms covered and then sautéing them uncovered allowed their excess moisture to evaporate before browning. Umami-rich anchovy fillets and garlic added depth to the soup while leek contributed further sweetness and body. Gently simmering the parsnips brought out their sweetness. White wine and white wine vinegar brightened up the dish and a little cream brought it all together. A generous amount of tarragon gave freshness to our balanced and hearty soup. To thaw the frozen artichokes quickly, microwave them on high, covered, for 3 to 5 minutes. Frozen artichokes are generally packaged already quartered; if yours are not, cut the artichoke hearts into quarters before using.

serves 4 to 6

3 tablespoons extra-virgin olive oil

18 ounces frozen artichoke hearts, thawed and patted dry

12 ounces white mushrooms, trimmed and sliced thin

1 leek, white and light green parts only, halved lengthwise, sliced 1/4 inch thick, and washed thoroughly

4 garlic cloves, minced

2 anchovy fillets, rinsed, patted dry, and minced

1 teaspoon minced fresh thyme or 1/4 teaspoon dried

3 tablespoons all-purpose flour

1/4 cup dry white wine

3 cups chicken broth

3 cups vegetable broth

6 ounces parsnips, peeled and cut into 1/2-inch pieces

2 bay leaves

Salt and pepper

1/4 cup heavy cream

2 tablespoons minced fresh tarragon

1 teaspoon white wine vinegar, plus extra for seasoning

1. Heat 1 tablespoon oil in Dutch oven over medium heat until shimmering. Add artichokes and cook until browned, 8 to 10 minutes. Transfer to cutting board, let cool slightly, then chop coarse.

2. Heat 1 tablespoon oil in now-empty pot over medium heat until shimmering. Add mushrooms, cover, and cook until they have released their liquid, about 5 minutes. Uncover and cook until mushrooms are dry, about 5 minutes longer.

3. Stir in leek and remaining 1 tablespoon oil and cook until leek is softened and mushrooms are browned, 8 to 10 minutes. Stir in garlic, anchovies, and thyme and cook until fragrant, about 30 seconds. Stir in flour and cook for 1 minute. Stir in wine, scraping up any browned bits, and cook until nearly evaporated, about 1 minute.

4. Gradually whisk in chicken broth and vegetable broth, smoothing out any lumps. Stir in browned artichokes, parsnips, bay leaves, and 1/2 teaspoon salt and bring to boil. Cover, reduce to gentle simmer, and cook until parsnips are tender, 15 to 20 minutes.

5. Off heat, remove bay leaves. Stir in cream, tarragon, and 1 teaspoon vinegar. Season with salt, pepper, and extra vinegar to taste and serve.

beet and wheat berry soup with dill cream

why this recipe works This recipe is a thoroughly modern, fresh, and vegetarian take on traditional hot borscht. To complement the earthy shredded beets, we swapped the usual waxy, starchy potatoes for fiber-loaded wheat berries. Toasting the wheat berries gave a rich, nutty flavor and a pleasant chewy consistency to the soup. To build a flavorful backbone, we sautéed onion, garlic, thyme, and tomato paste before stirring in the broth. Red wine vinegar, red cabbage, and a dash of cayenne helped to round out the flavor of the beets as well. A dollop of dill cream added tang to this satisfying and vitamin-packed soup. You can use the shredding disk of the food processor to grate the beets and carrot and to shred the cabbage. Do not use presteamed or quick-cooking wheat berries here, as they have a much shorter cooking time; be prepared to read the package carefully to determine what kind of wheat berries you are using.

serves 6

soup

⅔ cup wheat berries, rinsed

3 tablespoons vegetable oil

2 onions, chopped fine

4 garlic cloves, minced

1 teaspoon minced fresh thyme or ½ teaspoon dried

2 tablespoons tomato paste

¼ teaspoon cayenne pepper

8 cups vegetable broth

3 cups water

1½ cups shredded red cabbage

1 pound beets, trimmed, peeled, and shredded

1 small carrot, peeled and shredded

1 bay leaf

Salt and pepper

1 tablespoon red wine vinegar

dill cream

½ cup sour cream

¼ cup minced fresh dill

½ teaspoon salt

1. for the soup Toast wheat berries in Dutch oven over medium heat, stirring often, until fragrant and beginning to darken, about 5 minutes; transfer to bowl.

2. Heat oil in now-empty pot over medium heat until shimmering. Stir in onions and cook until softened, about 5 minutes. Stir in garlic and thyme and cook until fragrant, about 30 seconds. Stir in tomato paste and cayenne and cook until darkened slightly, about 2 minutes.

3. Stir in broth and water, scraping up any browned bits. Stir in toasted wheat berries, cabbage, beets, carrot, bay leaf, and ¾ teaspoon pepper, and bring to boil. Reduce heat to low and simmer until wheat berries are tender but still chewy and vegetables are tender, 45 minutes to 1¼ hours.

4. for the dill cream Meanwhile, combine all ingredients in bowl.

5. Off heat, discard bay leaf and stir in vinegar and 1 teaspoon salt. Season with additional salt and pepper to taste. Top individual portions with dill cream and serve.

vegetable shabu-shabu with sesame sauce

why this recipe works This traditional Japanese soup features chewy udon noodles, silky tofu, and tender vegetables in a simple, savory broth. *Shabu-shabu* is a hot-pot dish in which beef, vegetables, and tofu are simmered in broth and served with udon noodles and dipping sauces. We wanted a version without the meat (or the hot pot). The traditional dashi broth is made from glutamate-rich kombu seaweed and bonito (tuna) flakes. After a good deal of testing, we found that adding a second variety of seaweed (wakame), fish sauce, rice wine, and sugar replicated the fishy depth of the bonito. Shabu-shabu typically includes carrots, napa cabbage or bok choy, enoki or shiitake mushrooms, tofu, and chrysanthemum leaves. Luckily, the hard-to-find chrysanthemum leaves were not missed when omitted. We preferred bok choy to cabbage and the fuller flavor of shiitake mushrooms. A dollop of homemade sesame sauce was the perfect garnish. We prefer the flavor of red miso here, but white miso can be substituted.

serves 6 to 8

sesame sauce
¼ cup sesame seeds, toasted

2 tablespoons mayonnaise

1 tablespoon red miso

2 teaspoons lemon juice

2 teaspoons sugar

1 garlic clove, minced

½ teaspoon water

soup
8 ounces dried udon noodles

Salt

½ ounce kombu seaweed, rinsed

½ ounce wakame seaweed, rinsed

½ cup mirin

¼ cup fish sauce

1½ teaspoons sugar

3 heads baby bok choy (4 ounces each), sliced ⅛ inch thick

3 carrots, peeled and sliced ⅛ inch thick

14 ounces soft tofu, cut into ½-inch cubes

8 ounces shiitake mushrooms, stemmed and sliced thin

1. for the sesame sauce Stir all ingredients together in bowl until smooth.

2. for the soup Bring 2 quarts water to boil in large pot. Add udon noodles and 1½ teaspoons salt and cook, stirring often, until tender; drain and set aside.

3. Meanwhile, bring 9 cups water, kombu, and wakame to brief boil in large pot over medium heat. Remove from heat and discard seaweed.

4. Stir in mirin, fish sauce, and sugar and bring to simmer over medium heat. Stir in bok choy and carrots and simmer until crisp-tender, 2 to 4 minutes. Stir in tofu, mushrooms, and cooked noodles and let heat through, about 1 minute. Drizzle individual portions with sesame sauce and serve.

why this recipe works There is no denying the appeal of a great bowl of French onion soup, with its rich broth, caramelized onions, and nutty Gruyère-topped bread. For a rich soup, we caramelized the onions a full 2½ hours in the oven and then deglazed the pot several times with water, before adding a combination of chicken broth, beef broth, and more water. Sweet onions, such as Vidalia or Walla Walla, will make this recipe overly sweet. Use broiler-safe crocks and keep the rim of the bowls 4 to 5 inches from the broiler element to obtain a proper gratinée of melted, bubbly cheese. If using ordinary soup bowls, sprinkle the toasted bread slices with Gruyère and return them to the broiler on the baking sheet until the cheese melts, then float them on top of the soup along with a sprinkle of parsley.

serves 6

soup
4 pounds onions, halved and sliced through root end into ¼-inch-thick pieces

3 tablespoons unsalted butter, cut into 3 pieces

Salt and pepper

2 cups water, plus extra for deglazing as needed

½ cup dry sherry

4 cups chicken broth

2 cups beef broth

6 sprigs fresh thyme, tied with kitchen twine

1 bay leaf

cheese croutons
1 small baguette, cut into ½-inch slices

8 ounces Gruyère cheese, shredded (2 cups)

1. for the soup Adjust oven rack to lower-middle position and heat oven to 400 degrees. Generously spray inside of Dutch oven with vegetable oil spray. Add onions, butter, and 1 teaspoon salt. Cover and bake until onions wilt slightly and look moist, about 1 hour.

2. Stir onions thoroughly, scraping bottom and sides of pot. Partially cover pot and continue to cook in oven until onions are very soft and golden brown, 1½ to 1¾ hours longer, stirring onions thoroughly after 1 hour.

3. Carefully remove pot from oven and place over medium-high heat. Using oven mitts to handle pot, continue to cook onions, stirring and scraping pot often, until liquid evaporates, onions brown, and bottom of pot is coated with dark crust, 20 to 25 minutes. (If onions begin to brown too quickly, reduce heat to medium. Also, be sure to scrape any browned bits that collect on spoon back into onions.)

4. Stir in ¼ cup water, thoroughly scraping up browned crust. Continue to cook until water evaporates and pot bottom has formed another dark crust, 6 to 8 minutes. Repeat deglazing 2 or 3 more times, until onions are very dark brown.

5. Stir in sherry and cook until evaporated, about 5 minutes. Stir in chicken broth, beef broth, 2 cups more water, thyme bundle, bay leaf, and ½ teaspoon salt, scraping up any remaining browned bits. Bring to simmer, cover, and cook for 30 minutes. Discard thyme bundle and bay leaf and season with salt and pepper to taste. (Soup can be refrigerated for up to 3 days; return to simmer before proceeding.)

6. for the cheese croutons Adjust oven rack to middle position and heat oven to 400 degrees. Lay baguette slices on rimmed baking sheet and bake until dry, crisp, and lightly golden, about 10 minutes, flipping slices over halfway through baking.

7. Position oven rack 8 inches from broiler element and heat broiler. Set individual broiler-safe crocks on baking sheet and fill each with about 1½ cups soup. Top each bowl with 1 or 2 baguette slices (do not overlap slices) and sprinkle evenly with Gruyère. Broil until cheese is melted and bubbly around edges, 3 to 5 minutes. Let cool for 5 minutes before serving.

to make ahead
Pot of cooked onions in step 2 can be cooled, covered, and refrigerated for up to 3 days before continuing with step 3.

garlic-potato soup

why this recipe works The base of this deliciously simple soup is a hearty emulsion of leek, garlic, and potatoes blended with a little heavy cream. We used both peeled russet potatoes for the way they broke down and thickened the broth and unpeeled red potatoes for ultimate potato flavor. To incorporate great garlic flavor, we sautéed minced cloves in the base, simmered whole heads in the broth, and added a garnish of toasted garlic chips. A garnish is essential to add crunch and flavor to the soup. We liked Garlic Chips, but crisp bacon bits or Garlic Croutons (page 11) are good options, too. A potato masher can be used instead of an immersion blender to mash some of the potatoes right in the pot, though the consistency will not be as creamy. If leeks are not available, substitute an equal amount of yellow onion. We prefer the soup made with chicken broth, but vegetable broth can be substituted.

serves 6

3 tablespoons unsalted butter

1 medium leek, white and light green parts halved lengthwise, chopped small, and washed thoroughly

3 garlic cloves, minced, plus 2 whole heads garlic, rinsed, outer papery skins removed and top third of heads cut off and discarded

6–7 cups chicken broth

2 bay leaves

Salt and pepper

1½ pounds russet potatoes, peeled and cut into ½-inch cubes

1 pound red potatoes, unpeeled, cut into ½-inch cubes

½ cup heavy cream

1½ teaspoons minced fresh thyme

¼ cup minced fresh chives

Garlic Chips (recipe follows)

1. Melt butter in Dutch oven over medium heat. Add leeks and cook until softened, 5 to 8 minutes. Stir in minced garlic and cook until fragrant, about 1 minute. Add garlic heads, 6 cups broth, bay leaves, and ¾ teaspoon salt; partially cover pot and bring to simmer over medium-high heat. Reduce heat and simmer until garlic is very tender when pierced with tip of knife, 30 to 40 minutes. Add potatoes and continue to simmer, partially covered, until potatoes are tender, 15 to 20 minutes.

2. Discard bay leaves. Remove garlic heads and squeeze cooked garlic from skins into bowl. Mash garlic to smooth paste with fork.

3. Stir cream, thyme, and half of mashed garlic into soup; heat soup until hot, about 2 minutes. Taste soup; add remaining garlic paste if desired. Transfer 1½ cups potatoes and 1 cup broth to blender and process until smooth. (Process more potatoes for thicker consistency.) Return puree to pot and adjust consistency as desired with remaining broth. Season with salt and pepper to taste. Sprinkle individual portions with chives and garlic chips and serve.

to make ahead

After adding potatoes in step 1, return soup to brief simmer then remove pot from heat and let soup rest for 10 minutes. Portion soup into 2 containers and freeze for up to 1 month. Return frozen soup to pot and add 1 cup additional chicken broth; cover and reheat over medium-high heat, stirring occasionally, until soup is hot and potatoes are tender. Continue with step 2 of recipe as directed.

garlic chips
makes about ¼ cup

3 tablespoons olive oil

6 garlic cloves, sliced thin lengthwise

Salt

Heat oil and garlic in 10-inch skillet over medium-high heat. Cook, turning garlic frequently, until light golden brown, about 3 minutes. Using slotted spoon, transfer garlic to plate lined with paper towels; discard oil. Season with salt to taste.

classic gazpacho

why this recipe works Hand-cut vegetables marinated in seasoned vinegar are the key to this stellar gazpacho. Chopping the vegetables by hand ensured they retained their color and firm texture. Letting them sit briefly in a sherry vinegar marinade guaranteed well-seasoned vegetables, while a combination of tomato juice and ice cubes (which helped chill the soup) provided the right amount of liquid. Chilling our soup for a minimum of 4 hours was critical to allow the flavors to develop and meld. Use a Vidalia, Maui, or Walla Walla onion here. This recipe makes a large quantity because the leftovers are so good, but it can be halved if you prefer. Traditionally, diners garnish their gazpacho with more of the same diced vegetables that are in the soup, so cut some extra vegetables when you prepare those called for in the recipe. Serve with Garlic Croutons (page 11), chopped pitted black olives, chopped hard-cooked eggs, and finely diced avocados. For a finishing touch, serve in chilled bowls.

serves 8 to 10

1½ **pounds tomatoes, cored and cut into ¼-inch dice**

2 **red bell peppers, stemmed, seeded, and cut into ¼-inch dice**

2 **small cucumbers (1 cucumber peeled, both sliced lengthwise, seeded, and cut into ¼-inch dice)**

½ **small sweet onion or 2 large shallots, minced**

⅓ **cup sherry vinegar**

2 **garlic cloves, minced**

Salt and pepper

5 **cups tomato juice**

8 **ice cubes**

1 **teaspoon hot sauce (optional)**

Extra-virgin olive oil

1. Combine tomatoes, bell peppers, cucumbers, onion, vinegar, garlic, and 2 teaspoons salt in large (at least 4-quart) bowl and season with pepper to taste. Let stand until vegetables just begin to release their juices, about 5 minutes. Stir in tomato juice, ice cubes, and hot sauce, if using. Cover and refrigerate to blend flavors, at least 4 hours or up to 2 days.

2. Discard any unmelted ice cubes and season soup with salt and pepper to taste. Serve cold, drizzling individual portions with oil.

variation

spicy gazpacho with chipotle chile and lime

We recommend garnishing bowls of this spicy soup with finely diced avocado. If desired, reduce the amount of chipotles to make the soup less spicy.

Omit hot sauce. Add 2 tablespoons minced fresh cilantro, 1 tablespoon minced canned chipotle chile in adobo sauce, and 2 teaspoons grated lime zest plus 6 tablespoons juice (3 limes) with tomato juice and ice cubes.

elegant
purees

115   great carrot-ginger soup

116   creamy cauliflower soup

      curried cauliflower soup

119   best mushroom bisque

120   roasted red pepper soup with smoked paprika and cilantro cream

123   creamless creamy tomato soup

124   sweet potato soup

126   creamy butternut squash soup

      creamy butternut squash soup with fennel

      curried butternut squash and apple soup

      southwestern butternut squash soup

129   broccoli-cheese soup

131   shrimp bisque

      seafood bisque

132   lobster bisque

135   spanish chilled almond and garlic soup (white gazpacho)

136   chilled borscht

great carrot-ginger soup

why this recipe works For a soup that tastes like its namesakes, we used two forms of carrot and two forms of ginger. The flavors of carrot-ginger soup often get elbowed out with the addition of other vegetables, fruits, or dairy so we kept these additions to a minimum. With a combination of cooked carrots and carrot juice, we were able to get well-rounded, fresh carrot flavor. Using a mixture of grated fresh ginger and crystallized ginger gave us bright, refreshing ginger flavor with a moderate kick of heat. Finally, for a silky-smooth texture, we added a touch of baking soda to help break down the carrots and ginger, producing a perfectly creamy soup. We finished with some simple garnishes of sour cream and chopped chives to provide texture and tang. In addition to these accompaniments, serve the soup with Classic Croutons (page 11). See page 4 for more information about pureeing soup.

serves 6

2 tablespoons unsalted butter or vegetable oil

2 onions, chopped fine

¼ cup minced crystallized ginger

1 tablespoon grated fresh ginger

2 garlic cloves, peeled and smashed

Salt and pepper

1 teaspoon sugar

2 pounds carrots, peeled and sliced ¼ inch thick

4 cups water

1½ cups carrot juice

2 sprigs fresh thyme

½ teaspoon baking soda

1 tablespoon cider vinegar

Chopped chives

Sour cream

1. Melt butter in large saucepan over medium heat. Stir in onions, crystallized ginger, fresh ginger, garlic, 2 teaspoons salt, and sugar. Cook, stirring often, until onions are softened but not browned, 5 to 7 minutes.

2. Stir in carrots, water, ¾ cup carrot juice, thyme sprigs, and baking soda. Increase heat to high and bring to simmer. Reduce heat to medium-low, cover, and simmer gently until carrots are very tender, 20 to 25 minutes.

3. Discard thyme sprigs. Working in batches, process soup in blender until smooth, 1 to 2 minutes. Return pureed soup to clean pot and stir in vinegar and remaining ¾ cup carrot juice.

4. Return soup to brief simmer over medium heat. Season with salt and pepper to taste. Serve, garnishing individual bowls with chives and sour cream.

creamy cauliflower soup

why this recipe works This wonderfully creamy cauliflower soup does not use any cream, which tends to dull the cauliflower's delicate flavor. Instead, we relied on the cauliflower's low insoluble fiber content, which doesn't fully break down during cooking, to produce a velvety-smooth puree. To ensure that the cauliflower flavor remained at the forefront, we cooked the cauliflower in water instead of broth, skipped the spice rack entirely, and bolstered the soup with sautéed onion and leek. Cauliflower's flavor changes dramatically depending on how long you cook it. We added the cauliflower to the simmering water in two stages so that we got the grassy flavor of just-cooked cauliflower and the sweeter, nuttier flavor of longer-cooked cauliflower. Finally, we browned florets in butter and used both as a flavorful and elegant garnish. White wine vinegar may be substituted for the sherry vinegar. Be sure to thoroughly trim the cauliflower's core of green leaves and leaf stems, which can be fibrous and can contribute to a grainy texture in the soup.

serves 4 to 6

1 head cauliflower (2 pounds)

8 tablespoons unsalted butter, cut into 8 pieces

1 leek, white and light green parts only, halved lengthwise, sliced thin, and washed thoroughly

1 small onion, halved and sliced thin

Salt and pepper

4½–5 cups water

½ teaspoon sherry vinegar

3 tablespoons minced fresh chives

1. Pull off outer leaves of cauliflower and trim stem. Using paring knife, cut around core to remove; slice core thin and reserve. Cut heaping 1 cup of ½-inch florets from head of cauliflower; set aside. Cut remaining cauliflower crosswise into ½-inch-thick slices.

2. Melt 3 tablespoons butter in large saucepan over medium-low heat. Add leek, onion, and 1½ teaspoons salt. Cook, stirring often, until leek and onion are softened but not browned, about 7 minutes.

3. Add 4½ cups water, sliced core, and half of sliced cauliflower. Increase heat to medium-high and bring to simmer. Reduce heat to medium-low and simmer gently for 15 minutes. Add remaining sliced cauliflower and simmer until cauliflower is tender and crumbles easily, 15 to 20 minutes.

4. Meanwhile, melt remaining 5 tablespoons butter in 8-inch skillet over medium heat. Add reserved florets and cook, stirring often, until florets are golden brown and butter is browned and has nutty aroma, 6 to 8 minutes. Remove skillet from heat and use slotted spoon to transfer florets to small bowl. Toss florets with vinegar and season with salt to taste. Pour browned butter in skillet into separate bowl and reserve for garnishing.

5. Process soup in blender until smooth, about 45 seconds. Return pureed soup to clean pot, bring to brief simmer over medium heat, and adjust consistency with remaining water as needed (soup should have thick, velvety texture but should be thin enough to settle with flat surface after being stirred). Season with salt to taste. Serve, garnishing individual bowls with browned florets, drizzle of browned butter, chives, and pepper.

variation

curried cauliflower soup

Before adding water to saucepan, stir 1½ tablespoons grated fresh ginger and 1 tablespoon curry powder into vegetables and cook until fragrant, about 30 seconds. Substitute ½ teaspoon lime juice for sherry vinegar, and 2 scallions, sliced thin on bias, for chives. Stir ½ cup canned coconut milk and 1 tablespoon lime juice into pureed soup before serving.

best mushroom bisque

why this recipe works This creamy mushroom bisque is a far more sophisticated version of cream of mushroom soup with an indulgent velvety texture and robust mushroom flavor. Too often the abundance of dairy that gives a mushroom bisque its trademark richness obscures the flavor of the mushrooms. We wanted a silky texture but we wanted deep, earthy flavor, too. To achieve this we used three kinds of mushrooms: white, cremini, and shiitake. Because mushrooms will exude moisture without being cut, we cooked them whole in the microwave until they had released most of their liquid. The dehydrated mushrooms browned more efficiently in the pot, which we then deglazed with the reserved mushroom liquid. We kept additional ingredients to a minimum so as not to distract from the mushrooms' flavor. A mixture of egg yolks and cream whisked in at the end gave the soup a texture that was luxurious without being cloying. To complement the lush texture and rich woodsy flavor of the soup, we garnished each bowl with cream and a sprinkle of chives. See page 4 for more information about pureeing soup.

serves 6 to 10

1 pound white mushrooms, trimmed

8 ounces cremini mushrooms, trimmed

8 ounces shiitake mushrooms, stemmed

Kosher salt and pepper

2 tablespoons vegetable oil

1 small onion, chopped fine

1 sprig fresh thyme

2 tablespoons dry sherry

4 cups water

3½ cups chicken broth

⅔ cup heavy cream, plus extra for serving

2 large egg yolks

1 teaspoon lemon juice

Chopped fresh chives

1. Toss white mushrooms, cremini mushrooms, shiitake mushrooms, and 1 tablespoon salt together in large bowl. Cover with large plate and microwave, stirring every 4 minutes, until mushrooms have released their liquid and reduced to about one-third their original volume, about 12 minutes. Transfer mushrooms to colander set in second large bowl and drain well. Reserve liquid.

2. Heat oil in Dutch oven over medium heat until shimmering. Add mushrooms and cook, stirring occasionally, until mushrooms are browned and fond has formed on bottom of pot, about 8 minutes. Add onion, thyme sprig, and ¼ teaspoon pepper and cook, stirring occasionally, until onion is just softened, about 2 minutes. Add sherry and cook until evaporated. Stir in reserved mushroom liquid and cook, scraping up any browned bits. Stir in water and broth and bring to simmer. Reduce heat to low and simmer for 20 minutes.

3. Discard thyme sprig. Working in batches, process soup in blender until very smooth, 1½ to 2 minutes per batch. Return soup to now-empty pot. (Soup can be refrigerated for up to 2 days. Warm to 150 degrees before proceeding with recipe.)

4. Whisk cream and egg yolks together in medium bowl. Stirring slowly and constantly, add 2 cups soup to cream mixture. Stirring constantly, slowly pour cream mixture into simmering soup. Heat gently, stirring constantly, until soup registers 165 degrees (do not overheat). Stir in lemon juice and season with salt and pepper to taste. Serve immediately, garnishing each serving with 1 teaspoon extra cream and sprinkle of chives.

roasted red pepper soup with smoked paprika and cilantro cream

why this recipe works This silky pureed soup highlights the smoky and rich flavor of roasted red peppers. To concentrate that flavor, we started by broiling the peppers until they were charred and puffed. Next, we built an aromatic base for our soup with garlic, red onion, cumin, and smoked paprika. Sautéing some tomato paste and flour gave the soup intense umami flavor and a velvety thickness. Finally, we whisked in broth, added the roasted peppers, and simmered them until they were tender before whirring the soup smooth. For a garnish, we made a bright cilantro-lime cream to top our soup. The flavor of this soup depends on homemade roasted red peppers; do not substitute jarred red peppers. Keep your eye on the peppers as they broil in step 2; the broiling time may vary depending on the intensity of your broiler. Sweet paprika can be substituted for the smoked paprika if necessary. See page 4 for more information on pureeing soup.

serves 8

cilantro cream
¾ cup sour cream

¼ cup whole milk

1 tablespoon minced fresh cilantro

½ teaspoon grated lime zest plus 1 tablespoon juice

Salt and pepper

soup
8 red bell peppers, cored and flattened

1 tablespoon extra-virgin olive oil

2 garlic cloves, minced

1 red onion, chopped

½ teaspoon ground cumin

½ teaspoon smoked paprika

2 tablespoons tomato paste

1 tablespoon all-purpose flour

4 cups chicken or vegetable broth, plus extra as needed

1 bay leaf

½ cup half-and-half

2 tablespoons dry sherry

2 tablespoons minced fresh cilantro

Salt and pepper

1. **for the cilantro cream** Whisk all ingredients together in bowl and season with salt and pepper to taste. Cover and refrigerate until needed.

2. **for the soup** Adjust oven rack 3 inches from broiler element and heat broiler. Spread half of bell peppers, skin side up, onto aluminum foil–lined baking sheet. Broil until skin is charred and puffed but flesh is still firm, 8 to 10 minutes, rotating sheet halfway through broiling. Transfer broiled peppers to bowl, cover with plastic wrap or foil, and let steam until skins peel off easily, 10 to 15 minutes. Repeat with remaining peppers. Peel broiled peppers, discarding skins, and chop coarse.

3. Cook oil and garlic together in Dutch oven over low heat, stirring constantly, until garlic is foamy, sticky, and straw-colored, 8 to 10 minutes. Stir in onion, increase heat to medium, and cook until softened, 5 to 7 minutes.

4. Stir in cumin and paprika and cook until fragrant, about 30 seconds. Stir in tomato paste and flour and cook for 1 minute. Gradually whisk in chicken broth, smoothing out any lumps. Stir in bay leaf and chopped roasted peppers, bring to simmer, and cook until peppers are very tender, 5 to 7 minutes.

5. Discard bay leaf. Working in batches, puree soup in blender until smooth, 1 to 2 minutes. Return soup to clean pot and stir in half-and-half, sherry, and additional broth as needed to adjust consistency. Heat soup gently over low heat until hot (do not boil). Stir in cilantro and season with salt and pepper to taste. Serve, drizzling individual portions with cilantro cream.

creamless creamy tomato soup

why this recipe works A warm bowl of tomato soup brings out the kid in all of us. Our homemade version satisfies a grown-up palate with its creamy texture and fresh taste. We wanted a tomato soup that would have velvety smoothness and a bright tomato taste—without flavor-dulling cream. We started with canned tomatoes for their convenience and year-round availability. Sautéing an onion in olive oil ramped up the sweet notes of the tomatoes and a little brown sugar balanced the tomatoes' acidity. A surprise ingredient—slices of crustless white bread torn into pieces and blended into the soup—helped give our tomato soup luxurious body without adding cream. Make sure to purchase canned whole tomatoes in juice, not in puree. If half of the soup fills your blender by more than two-thirds, process the soup in three batches. For an even smoother soup, pass the pureed mixture through a fine-mesh strainer after blending it. Serve with Classic Croutons (page 11).

serves 6 to 8

¼ cup extra-virgin olive oil, plus extra for serving

1 onion, chopped fine

3 garlic cloves, minced

1 bay leaf

Pinch red pepper flakes (optional)

2 (28-ounce) cans whole peeled tomatoes

3 slices hearty white sandwich bread, crusts removed, torn into 1-inch pieces

1 tablespoon packed brown sugar

2 cups chicken or vegetable broth

2 tablespoons brandy (optional)

Salt and pepper

¼ cup minced fresh chives

1. Heat 2 tablespoons oil in Dutch oven over medium-high heat until shimmering. Add onion, garlic, bay leaf, and pepper flakes, if using. Cook, stirring often, until onion is translucent, 3 to 5 minutes. Stir in tomatoes and their juice. Using potato masher, mash until no pieces bigger than 2 inches remain. Stir in bread and sugar and bring soup to boil. Reduce heat to medium and cook, stirring occasionally, until bread is completely saturated and starts to break down, about 5 minutes. Discard bay leaf.

2. Transfer half of soup to blender. Add 1 tablespoon oil and puree until soup is smooth and creamy, 2 to 3 minutes. Transfer to large bowl and repeat with remaining soup and remaining 1 tablespoon oil. Return pureed soup to clean pot.

3. Stir in broth and brandy, if using. Return soup to boil and season with salt and pepper to taste. Serve, sprinkling individual bowls with chives and drizzling with oil.

sweet potato soup

why this recipe works What are the secrets to our creamy sweet potato soup with deep, earthy-sweet flavor? Use the peels and turn off the heat. We stripped away the nonessential ingredients, including broth, to make a silky, luxurious soup in which the sweet potatoes really stood out. The usual preparation of the potatoes involves boiling and then pureeing. Our way: Soak before boiling. However, the real key to intensifying the sweet potato flavor was to use only a minimal amount of flavor-diluting water. To do so, we let the sweet potatoes sit in hot water off the heat, which converted their starch content into sugar. Less starch meant we could use less water, keeping the sweet potato flavor in the forefront. Pureeing a quarter of the potato skins into the soup took advantage of an earthy-tasting compound they contain. In addition to the chives, serve the soup with one of our suggested garnishes below or with Buttery Rye Croutons (page 11). The garnish can be prepared during step 1 while the sweet potatoes stand in the water. See page 4 for more information about pureeing soup.

serves 4 to 6

4 tablespoons unsalted butter

1 shallot, sliced thin

4 sprigs fresh thyme

4$\frac{1}{4}$ cups water

2 pounds sweet potatoes, peeled, halved lengthwise, and sliced $\frac{1}{4}$ inch thick, $\frac{1}{4}$ of peels reserved

1 tablespoon packed brown sugar

$\frac{1}{2}$ teaspoon cider vinegar

Salt and pepper

Minced fresh chives

1. Melt butter in large saucepan over medium-low heat. Add shallot and thyme sprigs and cook until shallot is softened but not browned, about 5 minutes. Add water, increase heat to high, and bring to simmer. Remove pot from heat, add sweet potatoes and reserved peels, and let stand uncovered for 20 minutes.

2. Add sugar, vinegar, 1$\frac{1}{2}$ teaspoons salt, and $\frac{1}{4}$ teaspoon pepper. Bring to simmer over high heat. Reduce heat to medium-low, cover, and cook until potatoes are very soft, about 10 minutes.

3. Discard thyme sprigs. Working in batches, process soup in blender until smooth, 45 to 60 seconds. Return soup to clean pot. Bring to simmer over medium heat, adjusting consistency if desired. Season with salt and pepper to taste. Serve, topping each portion with sprinkle of chives.

candied bacon bits
makes about $\frac{1}{4}$ cup
Break up any large chunks before serving.

4 slices bacon, cut into $\frac{1}{2}$-inch pieces

2 teaspoons packed dark brown sugar

$\frac{1}{2}$ teaspoon cider vinegar

Cook bacon in 10-inch nonstick skillet over medium heat until crisp and well rendered, 6 to 8 minutes. Using slotted spoon, remove bacon from skillet and discard fat. Return bacon to skillet and add brown sugar and vinegar. Cook over low heat, stirring constantly, until bacon is evenly coated. Transfer to plate in single layer. Let bacon cool completely.

maple sour cream
makes $\frac{1}{3}$ cup
Maple balances the sweet potatoes' earthiness.

$\frac{1}{3}$ cup sour cream

1 tablespoon maple syrup

Combine ingredients in bowl.

creamy butternut squash soup

why this recipe works This simple butternut squash soup is little more than squash, cooking liquid, and a few aromatic ingredients; it comes together easily yet is creamy and deeply flavorful. Many squash soups fail to live up to their potential, often ending up too sweet or with too little squash flavor. We got the most flavor out of our squash by sautéing a shallot in butter with the reserved squash seeds and fibers, simmering the mixture in water, and then using the flavorful liquid to steam the unpeeled squash. This method gave us doubly flavorful, tender squash with the added bonus of avoiding the difficult task of peeling raw squash. To complete our soup, we scooped out the cooked squash from its skin and then pureed it with some of the strained steaming liquid for a perfectly smooth texture. Some heavy cream added richness, and a little brown sugar and nutmeg balanced the squash's earthy flavor. Serve with Cinnamon-Sugar Croutons (page 11).

serves 4 to 6

4 tablespoons unsalted butter, cut into ½-inch pieces

1 large shallot, chopped

3 pounds butternut squash, quartered and seeded, with fibers and seeds reserved

6 cups water

Salt and pepper

½ cup heavy cream

1 teaspoon packed dark brown sugar

Pinch ground nutmeg

1. Melt 2 tablespoons butter in Dutch oven over medium heat. Add shallot and cook until softened, 2 to 3 minutes. Stir in squash seeds and fibers and cook until butter turns orange, about 4 minutes.

2. Stir in water and 1 teaspoon salt and bring to boil. Reduce heat to simmer, place squash cut side down in steamer basket, and lower basket into pot. Cover and steam squash until completely tender, 30 to 40 minutes.

3. Using tongs, transfer cooked squash to rimmed baking sheet. Let squash cool slightly, then scrape cooked squash from skin using soupspoon; discard skin.

4. Strain cooking liquid through fine-mesh strainer into large liquid measuring cup. Working in batches, puree cooked squash with 3 cups strained cooking liquid in blender until smooth, 1 to 2 minutes. Return pureed soup to clean pot and stir in cream, sugar, nutmeg, and remaining 2 tablespoons butter. Return to brief simmer, adding additional strained cooking liquid as needed to adjust consistency. Season with salt and pepper to taste, and serve.

variations

creamy butternut squash soup with fennel
Reduce amount of squash to 2 pounds and add 1 teaspoon fennel seeds to pot with squash seeds and fibers. Add 1 large fennel bulb, cut into 1-inch-thick strips, to steamer basket with squash.

curried butternut squash and apple soup
A tart apple, such as a Granny Smith, adds a nice contrast to the sweet squash, but any type of apple may be used.

Reduce amount of squash to 2½ pounds. Add 1 large apple, peeled, cored, and quartered, to steamer basket with squash. Substitute 2 teaspoons curry powder for nutmeg.

southwestern butternut squash soup
Substitute 1 tablespoon honey for brown sugar and ½ teaspoon ground cumin for nutmeg. Stir 2 tablespoons minced fresh cilantro and 2 teaspoons minced canned chipotle chile in adobo sauce into soup before serving.

broccoli-cheese soup

why this recipe works It seems counterintuitive, but cooking the daylights out of the broccoli is the key to this soup's sweet, nutty vegetable flavor. Our first step was to call for a full 2 pounds of broccoli. Following a technique from renowned California chef Alice Waters, we sautéed the broccoli in a little butter, added a cup of water, and let it cook until it was very soft and nutty and sweet. We discovered that adding just a pinch of baking soda with the water accelerated the braising time by helping to break down the cell walls of the broccoli. Adding fresh baby spinach right before pureeing ensured that our soup had a bright color and it also enhanced the vegetable flavor. As for the cheese, a mix of sharp cheddar and nutty Parmesan gave the soup enough cheesy flavor and richness that we didn't need to use any cream. If you like, serve this soup with Classic Croutons (page 11).

2 tablespoons unsalted butter

2 pounds broccoli, florets cut into 1-inch pieces, stalks peeled and sliced ¼ inch thick

1 onion, chopped coarse

2 garlic cloves, minced

1½ teaspoons dry mustard powder

Pinch cayenne pepper

Salt and pepper

3–4 cups water

¼ teaspoon baking soda

2 cups chicken or vegetable broth

2 ounces (2 cups) baby spinach

3 ounces sharp cheddar cheese, shredded (¾ cup)

1½ ounces Parmesan cheese, grated fine (¾ cup), plus extra for serving

1. Melt butter in Dutch oven over medium-high heat. Add broccoli, onion, garlic, dry mustard, cayenne, and 1 teaspoon salt and cook, stirring frequently, until fragrant, about 6 minutes. Add 1 cup water and baking soda. Bring to simmer, cover, and cook until broccoli is very soft, about 20 minutes, stirring once during cooking.

2. Add broth and 2 cups water and increase heat to medium-high. When mixture begins to simmer, stir in spinach and cook until wilted, about 1 minute. Transfer half of soup to blender, add cheddar and Parmesan, and process until smooth, about 1 minute. Transfer soup to medium bowl and repeat with remaining soup. Return soup to pot, place over medium heat and bring to simmer. Adjust consistency of soup with up to 1 cup remaining water. Season with salt and pepper to taste. Serve, passing extra Parmesan separately.

shrimp bisque

why this recipe works Our stellar shrimp bisque is rich and velvety—delicate in character but deeply intense—with an almost sweet shrimp essence and an interplay of supporting flavors. Its texture is incredibly silky with tender pieces of poached shrimp. For incomparable shrimp flavor, we ground the shrimp shells and half the shrimp, simmered them, and then strained them from the broth. We added the remaining shrimp at the last minute as a garnish. Before flambéing, be sure to roll up long shirtsleeves, tie back long hair, and turn off the exhaust fan and any lit burners.

serves 6

2 pounds medium-large shrimp (31 to 40 per pound)

2 tablespoons vegetable oil

⅓ cup brandy or cognac, warmed

1 onion, chopped coarse

1 carrot, peeled and chopped coarse

1 celery rib, chopped coarse

1 garlic clove, peeled

2 tablespoons unsalted butter

½ cup all-purpose flour

1½ cups dry white wine

4 (8-ounce) bottles clam juice

1 (14.5-ounce) can diced tomatoes, drained

1 cup heavy cream

1 tablespoon lemon juice

1 small sprig fresh tarragon

Pinch ground cayenne

2 tablespoons dry sherry or Madeira

Salt and pepper

2 tablespoons minced fresh chives

1 recipe Butter Croutons (page 11)

1. Peel and devein 1 pound of shrimp, reserving shells, and cut each shrimp into 3 pieces; refrigerate until needed.

2. Heat oil in 12-inch skillet over medium-high heat until just smoking. Add remaining 1 pound shrimp and reserved shrimp shells and cook until lightly browned, 3 to 5 minutes. Add brandy and let warm through, about 5 seconds. Wave lit match over pan until brandy ignites, then shake pan to distribute flames.

3. Transfer flambéed shrimp mixture to food processor and process until mixture resembles fine meal, 10 to 20 seconds. Transfer to bowl. Pulse onion, carrot, celery, and garlic in food processor until finely chopped, about 5 pulses.

4. Melt butter in Dutch oven over medium heat. Add processed shrimp and vegetables, cover, and cook until softened and fragrant, 5 to 7 minutes. Stir in flour and cook for 1 minute.

5. Gradually stir in wine and clam juice, scraping up any browned bits and smoothing out any lumps. Stir in tomatoes and bring to boil. Reduce to gentle simmer and cook until thickened and flavors meld, about 20 minutes.

6. Strain broth through fine-mesh strainer, pressing on solids to release as much liquid as possible. Clean pot and return it to stove.

7. Add strained broth, cream, lemon juice, tarragon sprig, and cayenne to pot and bring to simmer. Stir in reserved shrimp pieces and gently simmer until shrimp are bright pink, 1 to 2 minutes. Off heat, discard tarragon sprig, stir in sherry, and season with salt and pepper to taste. Sprinkle individual portions with chives and croutons before serving.

variation

seafood bisque
Reduce shrimp to 8 ounces. Add 8 ounces large sea scallops, tendons removed, cut into quarters, to soup with reserved shrimp pieces in step 7. Add 8 ounces cooked lobster meat, cut into ½-inch pieces, to soup with sherry in step 7; cover, and let heat through before serving.

lobster bisque

why this recipe works This luxurious soup has chunks of lobster meat held in its silky-smooth, rich flavored cream base. First we steamed lobsters and removed the meat. To extract the most flavor, we ground the lobster shells and sautéed them. Next we flambéed the shells with brandy and added them to the steaming liquid, which was thickened and flavored with browned vegetables. For a classic presentation, float the meat from one claw in the center of each bowl. Before flambéing, be sure to roll up long shirt-sleeves, tie back long hair, and turn off the exhaust fan and any lit burners.

serves 6

1½ cups dry white wine

4 (8-ounce) bottles clam juice

3 (1-pound) live lobsters

2 tablespoons olive oil

¼ cup brandy or cognac, warmed

6 tablespoons unsalted butter

1 small carrot, chopped fine

1 small celery rib, chopped fine

1 small onion, chopped fine

1 garlic clove, minced

½ cup all-purpose flour

1 (14.5-ounce) can diced tomatoes, drained

½ teaspoon minced fresh tarragon, plus 1 small sprig

1 cup heavy cream

1 tablespoon lemon juice

Pinch ground cayenne

1 tablespoon dry sherry

Salt and pepper

1. Bring wine and 3 bottles clam juice to boil over high heat in large stockpot. Rinse lobsters then add to pot. Cover and steam lobsters for 3 minutes. Shake pot to redistribute lobsters and steam for 4 minutes longer. Transfer lobsters to bowl; let cool. Strain liquid through fine-mesh strainer into separate bowl.

2. Remove lobster meat from tail and claws and dice; place in bowl, cover, and refrigerate. Split lobster bodies in half lengthwise then remove and discard innards.

3. Grind shells in food processor in 2 or 3 batches. (Some pinkish paste may coat some of shells.) Heat oil in 12-inch skillet over high heat until just smoking, about 3 minutes. Add half of lobster shells and cook until lightly browned, about 3 minutes; transfer to bowl. Repeat with remaining oil and shells. Off heat, return all shells to skillet, add brandy, and let warm through, about 5 seconds. Wave lit match over pan until brandy ignites, then shake pan to distribute flames.

4. Meanwhile, melt 2 tablespoons butter in Dutch oven over medium heat. Add carrot, celery, onion, and garlic and cook until vegetables are softened and lightly browned, 6 to 7 minutes. Stir in remaining 4 tablespoons butter until melted. Stir in flour until thoroughly combined and cook for 1 minute. Slowly stir in strained steaming liquid, scraping up any browned bits and smoothing out any lumps. Add tomatoes, tarragon sprig, and lobster shells. Add remaining 1 bottle clam juice to now-empty skillet and bring to boil over high heat, scraping up browned bits; add to Dutch oven.

5. Bring soup to boil, then cover and reduce heat to low. Simmer gently, stirring often, until thickened, about 20 minutes. Stir in cream and simmer for 10 minutes longer.

6. Strain bisque through fine-mesh strainer into bowl, pressing on solids with back of ladle to extract all liquid. Wash and dry Dutch oven. Return strained bisque to Dutch oven and stir in lemon juice and cayenne. Bring soup to simmer over medium-high heat. When hot, add diced lobster meat and sherry and season with salt and pepper to taste. Serve immediately, garnishing each bowl with minced tarragon.

spanish chilled almond and garlic soup (white gazpacho)

why this recipe works Spanish white gazpacho is a very sophisticated cousin of the more familiar tomato-based version. Made with almonds, bread, and garlic, it is a study in contrasts: Some bites offer a nutty crunch, while others are sharply fruity and floral. But the versions we tried were watery and bland, or even grainy. We found that the order in which we added ingredients to the blender made all the difference. First, we ground almonds, then we added bread (which had been soaked briefly in water), garlic, sherry vinegar, salt, and cayenne pepper. Then we drizzled in olive oil and water. To get just a hint of almond flavor without overwhelming the soup, we mixed a tablespoon of the pureed soup with almond extract, then stirred a teaspoon of the mixture back into the soup. Sliced green grapes and toasted almonds added fruitiness and crunch. An extra drizzle of olive oil made for a rich finish and a beautiful presentation. This rich soup is best when served in small portions (about 6 ounces). Use a good-quality extra-virgin olive oil; our favorite premium oil is Columela Extra Virgin Olive Oil.

serves 6 to 8

6 slices hearty white sandwich bread, crusts removed

4 cups water

2½ cups (8¾ ounces) plus ⅓ cup sliced blanched almonds

1 garlic clove, peeled

3 tablespoons sherry vinegar

Salt and pepper

Pinch cayenne pepper

½ cup extra-virgin olive oil, plus extra for drizzling

⅛ teaspoon almond extract

2 teaspoons vegetable oil

6 ounces seedless green grapes, sliced thin (1 cup)

1. Combine bread and water in bowl and let soak for 5 minutes. Process 2½ cups almonds in blender until finely ground, about 30 seconds, scraping down sides of blender jar as needed. Using your hands, remove bread from water, squeeze it lightly, and transfer to blender with almonds. Measure out 3 cups soaking water and set aside; transfer remaining soaking water to blender. Add garlic, vinegar, ½ teaspoon salt, and cayenne to blender and process until mixture has consistency of cake batter, 30 to 45 seconds. With blender running, add olive oil in thin, steady stream, about 30 seconds. Add reserved soaking water and process for 1 minute.

2. Season with salt and pepper to taste. Strain soup through fine-mesh strainer set in bowl, pressing on solids to extract liquid. Discard solids.

3. Measure 1 tablespoon soup into separate bowl and stir in almond extract. Return 1 teaspoon extract-soup mixture to soup; discard remaining mixture. Chill soup for at least 3 hours or up to 24 hours.

4. Heat vegetable oil in 8-inch skillet over medium-high heat until oil begins to shimmer. Add remaining ⅓ cup almonds and cook, stirring constantly, until golden brown, 3 to 4 minutes. Immediately transfer to bowl and stir in ¼ teaspoon salt.

5. Ladle soup into shallow bowls. Mound grapes in center of each bowl, sprinkle with cooled almonds, and drizzle with extra olive oil. Serve immediately.

chilled borscht

serves 4 to 6

why this recipe works Hot borscht is a grand affair, but chilled borscht is much simpler, with the beets taking center stage. While developing our chilled borscht recipe, we found that cooking beets in water was the best method since it produced a liquid base on which to build a soup. We boiled whole beets until tender so they retained as much of their flavor as possible. We didn't bother peeling the beets until after cooking them; using a paper towel, we could rub the skins right off the cooked beets. We preferred the chilled borscht recipe made with water rather than stock, which overwhelmed the flavor of the beets. This soup has a brilliant, deep pink broth that is thick with strips of burgundy beets. The classic garnish of a little dill adds a bright green contrast. Many other garnish options can add flavor and color to this soup; see below for suggestions. If possible, buy beets with the greens attached. Fresh tops mean fresh beets, and boiling the beets with some stem attached makes it easy to peel them. Medium-size beets are best for this recipe. Small beets create more work, and large beets are sometimes tough.

2 pounds beets (6 medium), scrubbed and all but 1 inch of stems removed

1 small onion, peeled

¼ cup distilled white vinegar

¼ cup sugar

1½ teaspoons salt

¾ cup heavy cream

¾ cup sour cream

1 tablespoon lemon juice

2 tablespoons chopped fresh dill

1. Place 7 cups water, beets, onion, vinegar, sugar, and salt in large saucepan. Bring to boil over high heat. Reduce heat to medium-low, cover partially, and simmer until beets are tender and can be easily pierced with skewer, about 45 minutes.

2. Remove and discard onion. Transfer beets to cutting board and let cool slightly. Strain liquid through strainer lined with paper towel and reserve.

3. Using paper towel, rub skin from beets. Grate half of beets on large holes of box grater or food processor fitted with shredding disk. Refrigerate grated beets until cold. Cut remaining beets into large chunks. Place half of cut beets in blender. Add just enough cooking liquid to cover them by 1 inch and blend until very smooth, about 2 minutes. Transfer to large container. Repeat with remaining beets. Stir remaining cooking liquid into pureed beets and refrigerate until cold, about 2 hours.

4. Remove pureed beets and grated beets from refrigerator. Whisk heavy cream and sour cream into pureed beets until smooth and fully blended. Stir in grated beets. (Soup can be refrigerated in an airtight container for up to 3 days.) Stir in lemon juice and adjust seasonings. Ladle soup into bowls and garnish with dill and other garnishes as desired. Serve immediately.

garnishing borscht

Borscht lends itself to an assortment of garnishes that offer complementary flavor, texture, and color. Add one or two of the following garnishes (along with the dill) to each bowl of soup, or offer an assortment and let diners pick and choose as they like, garnishing their own bowls.

4 ounces small red potatoes, scrubbed, boiled until tender, and cut into ¼-inch dice

½ large cucumber, seeded and cut into ¼-inch dice

2 hard-cooked eggs, chopped fine

½ red onion, chopped fine

1 lemon, cut into wedges

rustic
bean
soups

140 hearty minestrone
143 pasta e fagioli
     with orange and fennel
144 tuscan white bean soup
     ribollita
146 hearty spanish-style lentil and chorizo soup
     with kale
149 curried vegetarian lentil soup
     with spinach
150 white lentil soup with coconut milk and mustard greens
153 sicilian chickpea and escarole soup
154 moroccan-style chickpea soup
157 hearty 15-bean and vegetable soup
158 black bean soup
     with chipotle chiles
160 u.s. senate navy bean soup
163 split pea and ham soup

hearty minestrone

why this recipe works A good minestrone captures the fleeting flavors of summer vegetables in a bowl. This recipe squeezes every last ounce of flavor out of the vegetables and features creamy dried beans and a surprisingly rich broth. Sautéing pancetta and then cooking the vegetables in the rendered fat gave our soup layers of flavor, while a Parmesan rind added richness. Starch from simmering beans thickened the soup. The last component we considered for our perfect minestrone was the liquid, settling on just the right combination of chicken broth, water, and V8 juice (which added a big wallop of vegetable flavor). If you're pressed for time, you can use our quick-salt-soak method for the beans that takes just 1 hour: In step 1, combine the salt, water, and beans in a Dutch oven and bring them to a boil over high heat. Remove the pot from the heat, cover, and let stand for 1 hour. Drain and rinse the beans and proceed with the recipe. We prefer cannellini beans, but navy or great Northern beans can be used. We prefer pancetta, but bacon can be used. For a spicier dish, use the larger amount of red pepper flakes. To make this soup vegetarian, substitute 2 teaspoons of olive oil for the pancetta and vegetable broth for the chicken broth. The Parmesan rind can be replaced with a 2-inch chunk of Parmesan cheese. In order for the starch from the beans to thicken the soup, it's important to maintain a vigorous simmer in step 3.

serves 6 to 8

Salt and pepper

8 ounces (1¼ cups) dried cannellini beans, picked over and rinsed

1 tablespoon extra-virgin olive oil, plus extra for serving

3 ounces pancetta, cut into ¼-inch pieces

2 celery ribs, cut into ½-inch pieces

2 small onions, cut into ½-inch pieces

1 carrot, peeled and cut into ½-inch pieces

1 zucchini, cut into ½-inch pieces

½ small head green cabbage, halved, cored, and cut into ½-inch pieces (2 cups)

2 garlic cloves, minced

⅛–¼ teaspoon red pepper flakes

2 cups chicken broth

1 Parmesan cheese rind, plus grated Parmesan for serving

1 bay leaf

1½ cups V8 juice

½ cup chopped fresh basil

1. Dissolve 1½ tablespoons salt in 2 quarts cold water in large container. Add beans and soak at room temperature for at least 8 hours or up to 24 hours. Drain and rinse well.

2. Heat oil and pancetta in Dutch oven over medium-high heat. Cook, stirring occasionally, until pancetta is lightly browned and fat has rendered, 3 to 5 minutes. Add celery, onions, carrot, and zucchini and cook, stirring frequently, until vegetables are softened and lightly browned, 5 to 9 minutes. Stir in cabbage, garlic, pepper flakes, and ½ teaspoon salt and continue to cook until cabbage starts to wilt, 1 to 2 minutes longer. Transfer vegetables to rimmed baking sheet and set aside.

3. Add soaked beans, 8 cups water, broth, Parmesan rind, and bay leaf to pot and bring to boil over high heat. Reduce heat and simmer vigorously, stirring occasionally, until beans are fully tender and liquid begins to thicken, 45 minutes to 1 hour.

4. Add reserved vegetables and V8 juice to pot and cook until vegetables are soft, about 15 minutes. Discard bay leaf and Parmesan rind, stir in basil, and season with salt and pepper to taste. Serve with extra oil and grated Parmesan. (Soup can be refrigerated for up to 2 days. Reheat gently and add basil just before serving.)

pasta e fagioli

why this recipe works This version of the classic Italian pasta and bean soup hits all the marks and delivers great flavor and perfect al dente texture without taking all afternoon. We started by cooking some pancetta (bacon worked well, too) in a Dutch oven and then cooked our vegetables in the rendered fat. Adding the tomatoes and beans together allowed them to absorb flavor from each other, and a 3:2 ratio of chicken broth to water added richness without turning our pasta and bean soup into chicken soup. We knew that adding a Parmesan rind to the pot would give our soup depth and a slight cheese flavor throughout (the rind can be replaced with a 2-inch chunk of cheese). Finally, parsley lent the necessary bright note to our soup. You can substitute another small pasta for the orzo, such as ditalini or tubettini.

serves 8 to 10

1 tablespoon extra-virgin olive oil, plus extra for serving

3 ounces pancetta or 3 slices bacon, chopped fine

1 onion, chopped fine

1 celery rib, chopped fine

4 garlic cloves, minced

1 teaspoon dried oregano

1/4 teaspoon red pepper flakes

3 anchovy fillets, rinsed and minced

1 (28-ounce) can diced tomatoes

2 (15-ounce) cans cannellini beans, rinsed

1 Parmesan cheese rind, plus grated Parmesan for serving

3 1/2 cups chicken broth

2 1/2 cups water

Salt and pepper

1 cup orzo

1/4 cup minced fresh parsley

1. Heat oil in Dutch oven over medium-high heat until shimmering. Add pancetta and cook, stirring often, until beginning to brown, 3 to 5 minutes. Stir in onion and celery and cook until vegetables are softened, 5 to 7 minutes. Stir in garlic, oregano, pepper flakes, and anchovies and cook until fragrant, about 1 minute.

2. Stir in tomatoes and their juice, scraping up any browned bits. Add beans and Parmesan rind. Bring to boil, then reduce heat to low and simmer to blend flavors, about 10 minutes.

3. Stir in broth, water, and 1 teaspoon salt. Increase heat to high and bring to boil. Add pasta and cook until al dente, about 10 minutes.

4. Discard Parmesan rind. Off heat, stir in parsley and season with salt and pepper to taste. Serve with extra olive oil and Parmesan.

variation

pasta e fagioli with orange and fennel
Ditalini and orzo are especially good pasta shapes for this variation.

Add 1 finely chopped fennel bulb to pot with onion and celery. Add 2 teaspoons grated orange zest and 1/2 teaspoon fennel seeds to pot with garlic.

tuscan white bean soup

why this recipe works This soup is a testament to restraint, comprised of only two components: tender, creamy beans and a broth perfumed with the fragrance of garlic and rosemary. We tossed out all the rules about how to prepare dried beans for this recipe. First, we skipped the presoak (soaked beans exploded once cooked), instead simmering them right in what would become the broth for our soup. We cooked them until just barely done and let residual heat gently cook them through to ensure even cooking. We also added salt to the pot, something typically thought to cause the beans' exteriors to toughen. We felt the salt actually helped keep the beans from bursting, and it also seasoned them nicely. Adding onion, garlic, bay leaf, and pancetta to our cooking broth gave the beans a welcome sweet and sour flavor. We liked the large size of cannellini beans. For a more authentic soup, place a small slice of lightly toasted Italian bread in the bottom of each bowl and ladle the soup over the bread. To make this soup vegetarian, omit the pancetta and add a piece of vegetarian Parmesan cheese rind to the pot along with the halved onion and unpeeled garlic in step 1.

serves 6 to 8

6 ounces pancetta, cut into 1-inch cubes

12 cups water, plus extra as needed

1 pound (2½ cups) dried cannellini beans, picked over and rinsed

1 large onion, unpeeled and halved, plus 1 small onion, chopped

4 garlic cloves, unpeeled, plus 3 garlic cloves, minced

1 bay leaf

Salt and pepper

¼ cup extra-virgin olive oil, plus extra for serving

1 sprig fresh rosemary

Balsamic vinegar

1. Cook pancetta in Dutch oven over medium heat until just golden, 8 to 10 minutes. Add water, beans, halved onion, unpeeled garlic cloves, bay leaf, and 1 teaspoon salt and bring to boil over medium-high heat. Cover partially, reduce heat to low, and simmer, stirring occasionally, until beans are almost tender, 1 to 1¼ hours. Remove pot from heat, cover, and let stand until beans are tender, about 30 minutes.

2. Drain beans in colander set over medium bowl, reserving cooking liquid (you should have about 5 cups; if not, add enough water to reach 5 cups). Discard pancetta, onion, unpeeled garlic cloves, and bay leaf. Spread beans in even layer on rimmed baking sheet and let cool.

3. While beans are cooling, heat oil in pot over medium heat until shimmering. Add chopped onion and cook, stirring occasionally, until softened, 5 to 6 minutes. Stir in minced garlic and cook until fragrant, about 30 seconds. Add cooled beans and reserved cooking liquid. Increase heat to medium-high and bring to simmer. Submerge rosemary in liquid, cover, and let stand off heat for 15 to 20 minutes. Season with salt and pepper to taste. Ladle soup into bowls, drizzle with olive oil, and serve, passing vinegar separately.

variation

ribollita

Don't be put off by its strange appearance—what ribollita lacks in beauty it makes up for in flavor. Be sure to use good-quality artisan or rustic bread.

Reheat leftover soup over medium-low heat until warm. Submerge slices of rustic day-old bread until completely softened, then blend or mash mixture until very thick.

hearty spanish-style lentil and chorizo soup

why this recipe works Like the Spanish *sopa de lentejas con chorizo* (lentil and chorizo soup), this sustaining soup economically pairs dried lentils with flavor-packed sausage. It's a standout not just for its robust taste—provided by rich, garlicky chorizo, heady smoked paprika, and the bright depth of sherry vinegar—but also for its unique texture: Neither entirely brothy nor creamy, the soup features whole lentils suspended in a thick broth. We prefer French green lentils, or *lentilles du Puy*, for this recipe, but it will work with any type of lentil except red or yellow. If Spanish-style chorizo is not available, kielbasa sausage can be substituted. Red wine vinegar can be substituted for the sherry vinegar. Smoked paprika comes in three varieties: sweet, bittersweet or medium hot, and hot. For this recipe, we prefer the sweet kind.

serves 6 to 8

1 pound (2¼ cups) lentils, picked over and rinsed

Salt and pepper

1 large onion

5 tablespoons extra-virgin olive oil

1½ pounds Spanish-style chorizo sausage, pricked with fork several times

3 carrots, peeled and cut into ¼-inch pieces

3 tablespoons minced fresh parsley

3 tablespoons sherry vinegar, plus extra for seasoning

2 bay leaves

⅛ teaspoon ground cloves

2 tablespoons sweet smoked paprika

3 garlic cloves, minced

1 tablespoon all-purpose flour

1. Place lentils and 2 teaspoons salt in heatproof container. Cover with 4 cups boiling water and let soak for 30 minutes. Drain well.

2. Meanwhile, finely chop three-quarters of onion (you should have about 1 cup) and grate remaining quarter (you should have about 3 tablespoons). Heat 2 tablespoons oil in Dutch oven over medium heat until shimmering. Add chorizo and cook until browned on all sides, 6 to 8 minutes. Transfer chorizo to large plate. Reduce heat to low and add chopped onion, carrots, 1 tablespoon parsley, and 1 teaspoon salt. Cover and cook, stirring occasionally, until vegetables are very soft but not brown, 25 to 30 minutes. If vegetables begin to brown, add 1 tablespoon water to pot.

3. Add lentils and vinegar to vegetables; increase heat to medium-high; and cook, stirring frequently, until vinegar starts to evaporate, 3 to 4 minutes. Add 7 cups water, chorizo, bay leaves, and cloves; bring to simmer. Reduce heat to low, cover, and cook until lentils are tender, about 30 minutes.

4. Heat remaining 3 tablespoons oil in small saucepan over medium heat until shimmering. Add paprika, grated onion, garlic, and ½ teaspoon pepper; cook, stirring constantly, until fragrant, 2 minutes. Add flour and cook, stirring constantly, 1 minute longer. Remove chorizo and bay leaves from lentils. Stir paprika mixture into lentils and continue to cook until flavors have blended and soup has thickened, 10 to 15 minutes. When chorizo is cool enough to handle, cut in half lengthwise, then cut each half into ¼-inch-thick slices. Return chorizo to soup along with remaining 2 tablespoons parsley and heat through, about 1 minute. Season with salt, pepper, and up to 2 teaspoons vinegar to taste, and serve.

variation

hearty spanish-style lentil and chorizo soup with kale
Add 12 ounces kale, stemmed and cut into ½-inch pieces, to simmering soup after 15 minutes in step 3. Continue to simmer until lentils and kale are tender, about 15 minutes.

curried vegetarian lentil soup

why this recipe works This simple and appealing soup takes complete advantage of the delicate, firm-tender bite and deep, earthy flavor of properly prepared lentils. We started by sautéing plenty of aromatics; we then added the lentils and cooked them until the vegetables were softened and the lentils had darkened, which helped them hold their shape and boosted their flavor. We deglazed the pan with white wine before adding the broth and water and simmering the lentils until tender. Pureeing part of the soup ensured that the broth had a luscious consistency. *Lentilles du Puy*, also called French green lentils, are our first choice for this recipe, but brown, black, or regular green lentils will work (note that cooking times will vary depending on the type used).

serves 4 to 6

2 tablespoons extra-virgin olive oil

1 large onion, chopped fine

2 carrots, peeled and chopped

3 garlic cloves, minced

1 teaspoon curry powder

1 (14.5-ounce) can diced tomatoes, drained

1 bay leaf

1 teaspoon minced fresh thyme

1 cup lentils, picked over and rinsed

Salt and pepper

½ cup dry white wine

4½ cups vegetable broth

1½ cups water

3 tablespoons minced fresh parsley

1. Heat oil in Dutch oven over medium-high heat until shimmering. Stir in onion and carrots and cook until vegetables begin to soften, about 2 minutes. Stir in garlic and curry powder and cook until fragrant, about 30 seconds. Stir in tomatoes, bay leaf, and thyme and cook until fragrant, about 30 seconds. Stir in lentils and ¼ teaspoon salt. Cover, reduce heat to medium-low, and cook until vegetables are softened and lentils have darkened, 8 to 10 minutes.

2. Uncover, increase heat to high, add wine, scraping up any browned bits, and bring to simmer. Stir in broth and water and bring to boil. Partially cover pot, reduce heat to low, and simmer until lentils are tender but still hold their shape, 30 to 35 minutes.

3. Discard bay leaf. Puree 3 cups soup in blender until smooth, then return to pot. Warm soup over medium-low heat until hot, about 5 minutes. Stir in parsley and serve.

variation

curried vegetarian lentil soup with spinach
Substitute 5 cups baby spinach for parsley; cook spinach in soup, stirring often, until wilted, about 3 minutes.

white lentil soup with coconut milk and mustard greens

serves 4

why this recipe works Our inspiration for this soup came from the spicy, largely vegetarian cuisine of southern India, which uses a lot of garlic, chiles, ginger, and coconut milk. White lentils, used throughout India in stews as well as ground into flour for dumplings and thin crêpes, have a particularly delicate flavor and cook down to a thick, creamy texture in this very flavorful soup. Mustard greens provided the perfect foil for the creamy soup base. We preferred the softer texture and milder flavor of the greens when we wilted them briefly in the microwave before stirring them into the finished soup. For a bright, fresh garnish, we made a chutney-inspired blend of diced fresh tomatoes, lime juice, and toasted whole cumin seeds. Be sure to rinse the white lentils well—they can come coated in a thin layer of oil. White lentils can be found in well-stocked supermarkets, specialty Indian markets, and online. If you can't find white lentils, substitute *lentilles du Puy* (French green lentils); reduce the lentil cooking time to 25 minutes and note that the soup will be more brothy.

2 teaspoons cumin seeds

3 tablespoons vegetable oil

1 onion, chopped fine

Salt and pepper

2 jalapeño chiles, stemmed, seeded, and minced

2 tablespoons grated fresh ginger

4 garlic cloves, minced

5½ cups vegetable broth

1 cup white lentils, picked over and rinsed

1 bay leaf

½ teaspoon turmeric

14 ounces mustard greens, stemmed and chopped

3 plum tomatoes, cored and chopped fine

1 tablespoon lime juice

¾ cup canned coconut milk

1. Toast cumin in 8-inch skillet over medium heat until fragrant, about 1 minute; transfer to bowl.

2. Heat oil in Dutch oven over medium heat until shimmering. Add onion and ½ teaspoon salt and cook until onion is softened and lightly browned, 5 to 7 minutes. Stir in half of jalapeño, ginger, and garlic and cook until fragrant and beginning to brown, about 3 minutes. Stir in broth, lentils, bay leaf, turmeric, and 1 teaspoon toasted cumin and bring to simmer. Reduce heat to low, partially cover, and simmer until lentils are tender, 40 to 50 minutes.

3. Meanwhile, microwave mustard greens in bowl until wilted and tender, 3 to 4 minutes; transfer to colander and let drain. In separate bowl, toss tomatoes, lime juice, remaining 1 teaspoon toasted cumin, remaining jalapeño, and ¼ teaspoon salt.

4. Discard bay leaf from soup. Puree ¾ cup soup and coconut milk in blender until smooth, about 30 seconds, then return to pot. Stir in mustard greens and bring to brief simmer. Season with salt and pepper to taste. Top individual portions with tomato mixture, and serve.

why this recipe works In Sicily, chickpeas are the favored legume to use in soup. In this version the mild bean shares the stage with escarole. We knew that dried chickpeas were the way to go for our traditional soup because we could infuse them with lots of flavor as they cooked. For aromatics, we started with the classic flavors of the region: onion, garlic, oregano, and red pepper flakes. We also added fennel, which grows wild throughout Sicily; its mild anise bite complemented the nutty chickpeas. A strip of orange zest added a subtle citrus note, while a Parmesan rind bolstered the chickpeas' flavor with a nutty richness and complexity. When stirred in for the last 5 minutes of cooking, the escarole leaves wilted until velvety and the stems retained a slight crunch. To speed up the process if you're tight on time, you can use our quick-salt-soak method for the beans: In step 1, combine the salt, water, and chickpeas in a Dutch oven and bring them to a boil over high heat. Remove the pot from the heat, cover, and let stand for 1 hour. Drain and rinse the beans and proceed with the recipe. The Parmesan rind can be replaced with a 2-inch chunk of the cheese. Serve with Garlic Toasts (page 11).

serves 6 to 8

Salt and pepper

1 pound (2¾ cups) dried chickpeas, picked over and rinsed

2 tablespoons extra-virgin olive oil, plus extra for serving

2 fennel bulbs, stalks discarded, bulbs halved, cored, and chopped fine

1 small onion, chopped

5 garlic cloves, minced

2 teaspoons minced fresh oregano or ½ teaspoon dried

¼ teaspoon red pepper flakes

5 cups vegetable broth

1 Parmesan cheese rind, plus grated Parmesan for serving

2 bay leaves

1 (3-inch) strip orange zest

1 head escarole (1 pound), trimmed and cut into 1-inch pieces

1 large tomato, cored and chopped

1. Dissolve 3 tablespoons salt in 4 quarts cold water in large container. Add chickpeas and soak at room temperature for at least 8 hours or up to 24 hours. Drain and rinse well.

2. Heat oil in Dutch oven over medium heat until shimmering. Add fennel, onion, and 1 teaspoon salt and cook until vegetables are softened, 7 to 10 minutes. Stir in garlic, oregano, and pepper flakes and cook until fragrant, about 30 seconds.

3. Stir in 7 cups water, broth, drained chickpeas, Parmesan rind, bay leaves, and orange zest and bring to boil. Reduce to gentle simmer and cook until chickpeas are tender, 1¼ to 1¾ hours.

4. Stir in escarole and tomato and cook until escarole is wilted, 5 to 10 minutes.

5. Off heat, remove bay leaves and Parmesan rind (scraping off any cheese that has melted and adding it back to pot). Season with salt and pepper to taste. Sprinkle individual portions with grated Parmesan, drizzle with extra oil, and serve.

why this recipe works This satisfyingly hearty and easy-to-make chickpea soup is infused with rich, complex Moroccan flavors. To make this soup easy, we used convenient canned chickpeas. Sautéing the onion with a little sugar sped up its cooking, and we added a substantial amount of garlic to the pot with paprika, saffron, ginger, and cumin for a potent aromatic flavor base. The saffron lent the soup a distinct aroma and rich color, while the cumin and ginger added a pungent kick that would fool anyone into thinking this soup had cooked for hours. Once the spices were fragrant, we added the chickpeas along with potatoes, canned diced tomatoes, and chopped zucchini. After just 20 minutes of simmering, the vegetables were tender and the rich flavors of the soup had melded. Mashing some of the potatoes into the soup helped to give it a rich consistency. You can substitute regular paprika and a pinch of cayenne for the hot paprika. Serve with plenty of hot sauce.

serves 4 to 6

3 tablespoons unsalted butter or extra-virgin olive oil

1 onion, chopped fine

1 teaspoon sugar

Salt and pepper

4 garlic cloves, minced

$\frac{1}{2}$ teaspoon hot paprika

$\frac{1}{4}$ teaspoon saffron threads, crumbled

$\frac{1}{4}$ teaspoon ground ginger

$\frac{1}{4}$ teaspoon ground cumin

2 (15-ounce) cans chickpeas, rinsed

1 pound red potatoes, unpeeled and cut into $\frac{1}{2}$-inch pieces

1 (14.5-ounce) can diced tomatoes

1 zucchini, cut into $\frac{1}{2}$-inch pieces

$3\frac{1}{2}$ cups vegetable broth

$\frac{1}{4}$ cup minced fresh parsley and/or mint

Lemon wedges

1. Melt butter in Dutch oven over medium-high heat. Add onion, sugar, and $\frac{1}{2}$ teaspoon salt and cook until onion is softened, about 5 minutes. Stir in garlic, paprika, saffron, ginger, and cumin and cook until fragrant, about 30 seconds. Stir in chickpeas, potatoes, tomatoes and their juice, zucchini, and broth. Simmer, stirring occasionally, until potatoes are tender, 20 to 30 minutes.

2. Using wooden spoon, mash some of potatoes against side of pot to thicken soup. Off heat, stir in parsley and season with salt and pepper to taste. Serve with lemon wedges.

hearty 15-bean and vegetable soup

why this recipe works This recipe coaxes a wide variety of beans to cook evenly and all complement each other. Bean soup mixes promise a shortcut to a flavorful bean soup, but the results are invariably disappointing. Different beans cook at different rates, leaving some blown-out and disintegrating while others remain hard. We wanted to doctor up a mix with fresh flavors and a smarter technique. To get the various beans to cook evenly, we started by brining them to soften their skins, preventing blowouts. Then we brought the soup to a simmer before transferring it to the oven to cook gently in the low, constant heat. To build depth and add a touch of smokiness we sautéed bacon with plenty of aromatics and added thyme, bay leaves, and savory dried porcini. Swiss chard, white mushrooms, and fresh tomato balanced the hearty beans. You can find 15-bean soup mix alongside the other bagged dried beans in the supermarket; any 1-pound bag of multiple varieties of beans will work in this recipe. The different varieties of beans cook at different rates, so be sure to taste several beans to ensure they are all tender before serving. To make this soup vegetarian, replace the bacon with 2 tablespoons extra-virgin olive oil and the chicken broth with vegetable broth. Heat the oil in a Dutch oven until shimmering then proceed with stirring in the onion and other vegetables in step 2.

serves 8 to 10

Salt and pepper

1 pound 15-bean soup mix, flavoring pack discarded, beans picked over and rinsed

4 slices bacon, chopped fine

1 small onion, chopped

1 carrot, peeled and chopped fine

1 pound Swiss chard, stems chopped, leaves sliced ½ inch thick

½ ounce dried porcini mushrooms, rinsed and minced

12 ounces white mushrooms, trimmed and quartered

6 garlic cloves, minced

2 teaspoons minced fresh thyme or ½ teaspoon dried

8 cups chicken broth

2 bay leaves

1 large tomato, cored and chopped

1. Dissolve 3 tablespoons salt in 4 quarts cold water in large container. Add beans and soak at room temperature for at least 8 hours or up to 24 hours. Drain and rinse well.

2. Adjust oven rack to lower-middle position and heat oven to 250 degrees. Cook bacon in Dutch oven over medium heat until crisp, 5 to 7 minutes. Stir in onion, carrot, chard stems, and porcini mushrooms and cook until vegetables are softened, 7 to 10 minutes.

3. Stir in white mushrooms, cover, and cook until mushrooms have released their liquid, about 5 minutes. Uncover and continue to cook until mushrooms are dry and browned, 5 to 10 minutes.

4. Stir in garlic and thyme and cook until fragrant, about 30 seconds. Stir in broth, soaked beans, and bay leaves and bring to boil. Cover pot, transfer to oven, and cook until beans are almost tender, 1 to 1¼ hours.

5. Stir in chard leaves and tomato and continue to cook in oven, covered, until beans and vegetables are fully tender, 30 to 40 minutes. Remove pot from oven and discard bay leaves. Season with salt and pepper to taste, and serve.

black bean soup

why this recipe works Our great black bean soup carefully balances sweet, spicy, and smoky flavors. To create a foolproof soup with beans that were tender, we went with dried beans, which released flavor into the broth as they cooked. Furthermore, they proved to be a timesaver: We discovered that we didn't need to soak the beans overnight or quick-soak them to make them tender. And we didn't need from-scratch stock; we maximized flavor by using water and store-bought chicken broth enhanced with ham and seasonings. Since ham hocks are mostly bone, we chose untraditional (for black bean soup) ham steak for smoky pork flavor along with plenty of meat. Dried beans tend to cook unevenly, so taste several beans to determine their doneness in step 1. For efficiency, you can prepare the soup ingredients while the beans simmer, and the garnishes while the soup simmers. Garnishes are essential for this soup, as they add not only flavor but texture and color as well. Serve with lime wedges, minced fresh cilantro, finely diced red onion, diced avocado, and sour cream.

serves 6

beans
1 pound (2½ cups) dried black beans, picked over and rinsed

5–6 cups water

4 ounces ham steak, trimmed

2 bay leaves

1 teaspoon salt

⅛ teaspoon baking soda

soup
3 tablespoons olive oil

2 large onions, chopped fine

3 celery ribs, chopped fine

1 large carrot, peeled and chopped fine

½ teaspoon salt

5–6 garlic cloves, minced

1½ tablespoons ground cumin

½ teaspoon red pepper flakes

6 cups chicken broth

2 tablespoons cornstarch

2 tablespoons water

2 tablespoons lime juice

Salt and pepper

1. for the beans Combine beans, 5 cups water, ham, bay leaves, salt, and baking soda in large saucepan. Bring to boil, skimming any impurities that rise to surface. Cover, reduce heat to low, and simmer gently until beans are tender, 1¼ to 1½ hours. (If after 1½ hours beans are not tender, add remaining 1 cup water and continue to simmer until beans are tender.) Discard bay leaves. Transfer ham steak to carving board and cut into ¼-inch pieces; set aside. (Do not drain beans.)

2. for the soup Heat oil in Dutch oven over medium heat until shimmering. Add onions, celery, carrot, and salt and cook until vegetables are softened and lightly browned, 12 to 15 minutes.

3. Stir in garlic, cumin, and pepper flakes and cook until fragrant, about 1 minute. Stir in broth and cooked beans with their cooking liquid, and bring to boil. Reduce heat to medium-low and cook, uncovered and stirring occasionally, until flavors have blended, about 30 minutes.

4. Puree 1½ cups of beans and 2 cups of liquid in blender until smooth, then return to pot. Whisk cornstarch and water together in small bowl, then gradually stir half of cornstarch mixture into simmering soup. Continue to simmer soup, stirring occasionally, until slightly thickened, 3 to 5 minutes. (If at this point soup is thinner than desired, repeat with remaining cornstarch mixture.) Off heat, stir in lime juice and reserved ham, season with salt and pepper to taste, and serve. (Soup can be refrigerated for up to 3 days. Add water as needed when reheating to adjust consistency.)

variation
black bean soup with chipotle chiles

Chipotle chiles are spicy; for a spicier soup, use the greater amount of chipotles given.

Omit red pepper flakes. Add 1 to 2 tablespoons minced canned chipotle chile in adobo sauce to soup with chicken broth.

u.s. senate navy bean soup

why this recipe works This simple, filling white bean and potato soup is a classic; it's been on the menu in the U.S. Senate dining room for more than a century. The original recipe derives much of its flavor from a ham hock, aromatic vegetables, and butter. We wanted to stay true to the simple ingredient list but ramp up the flavor. First, we doubled up on ham hocks. Next, we substituted vegetable oil for the butter so the vegetable flavor was cleaner. A few whole cloves, removed before serving the soup, added a gentle infusion of spice. And instead of stirring precooked mashed potatoes into the beans, as some recipes suggest, we added cut-up potatoes right to the soup pot and then mashed them to thicken the soup. The finished texture of the soup should be creamy but not too thick. We use whole cloves because ground cloves turn the soup an unsightly gray color.

serves 6 to 8

Salt and pepper

1 pound (2½ cups) navy beans, picked over and rinsed

1 tablespoon vegetable oil

1 onion, chopped fine

2 celery ribs, chopped fine

2 garlic cloves, minced

3 whole cloves

2 (12-ounce) smoked ham hocks

8 ounces russet potatoes, peeled and cut into ¼-inch pieces

1 tablespoon cider vinegar

1. Dissolve 3 tablespoons salt in 4 quarts cold water in large container. Add beans and soak at room temperature for at least 8 hours or up to 24 hours. Drain and rinse well.

2. Heat oil in Dutch oven over medium heat until shimmering. Add onion, celery, and 1 teaspoon salt and cook until softened, 8 to 10 minutes. Stir in garlic and cook until fragrant, about 30 seconds. Transfer onion mixture to bowl.

3. Insert cloves into skin of 1 ham hock. Add 8 cups water, ham hocks, and beans to now-empty pot and bring to boil over high heat. Reduce heat to medium-low and simmer, covered with lid slightly ajar, until beans are tender, 45 minutes to 1 hour, stirring occasionally.

4. Stir potatoes and onion mixture into soup and simmer, uncovered, until potatoes are tender, 10 to 15 minutes; remove pot from heat. Transfer ham hocks to cutting board and let cool slightly. Discard cloves, then shred meat, discarding bones and skin.

5. Using potato masher, gently mash beans and potatoes until soup is creamy and lightly thickened, 8 to 10 strokes. Add ½ teaspoon pepper and shredded meat and return to simmer over medium heat. Stir in vinegar. Season with salt and pepper to taste. Serve.

split pea and ham soup

why this recipe works This split pea soup has depth and lots of meaty flavor—without requiring a leftover ham bone. We set out to create a richly flavorful broth with tender shreds of meat. As it turns out, ham steak was plenty meaty and provided the soup with full pork flavor without making the soup too greasy. A few strips of raw thick-cut bacon added the richness and smokiness that the ham bone would have provided. (Four ounces of regular sliced bacon can be used, but the thinner slices are harder to remove from the soup.) Unsoaked peas broke down just as well as soaked and were better at absorbing the flavor of the soup. Depending on the age and brand of split peas, the consistency of the soup may vary slightly. If the soup is too thin at the end of step 2, increase the heat and simmer, uncovered, until the desired consistency is reached. If it is too thick, thin it with a little water. We like to garnish the soup with fresh peas, chopped mint, and a drizzle of aged balsamic vinegar. Serve with Classic Croutons (page 11).

serves 6 to 8

2 tablespoons unsalted butter

1 large onion, chopped fine

Salt and pepper

2 garlic cloves, minced

7 cups water

1 pound ham steak, skin removed, cut into quarters

1 pound (2½ cups) split peas, picked over and rinsed

3 slices thick-cut bacon

2 sprigs fresh thyme

2 bay leaves

2 carrots, peeled and cut into ½-inch pieces

1 celery rib, cut into ½-inch pieces

1. Melt butter in Dutch oven over medium-high heat. Add onion and ½ teaspoon salt and cook, stirring often, until onion is softened, 3 to 4 minutes. Stir in garlic and cook until fragrant, about 30 seconds. Stir in water, ham steak, peas, bacon, thyme sprigs, and bay leaves. Increase heat to high and bring to simmer, stirring frequently to keep peas from sticking to bottom. Reduce heat to low, cover, and simmer until peas are tender but not falling apart, about 45 minutes.

2. Remove ham steak and cover with plastic wrap to prevent it from drying out; set aside. Stir in carrots and celery and simmer, covered, until vegetables are tender and peas have almost completely broken down, about 30 minutes.

3. Shred ham into small bite-size pieces. Discard thyme sprigs, bay leaves, and bacon slices. Return ham to soup and season with salt and pepper to taste. Serve. (Soup can be refrigerated for up to 3 days. Add water as needed when reheating to adjust consistency.)

stocks
and
broths

167   classic chicken stock
168   rich beef stock
170   cheater chicken broth
171   cheater beef broth
173   beef bone broth
174   vegetable broth base

classic chicken stock

why this recipe works There are as many recipes to make chicken stock as there are cooks, but great homemade chicken stock is like liquid gold. It can improve everything you cook with it, not only soup but also risotto, bean dishes, sauces, and more. This stock delivers rich flavor and full body with almost no hands-on work. Our classic approach to making chicken stock calls for gently simmering a mix of chicken backs and wings in water for several hours. The long, slow simmer helped the bones and meat release both deep flavor and gelatin, which created a viscous consistency. We chose a combination of backs and wings not only for their convenience (they didn't need to be hacked into smaller pieces), but because, in addition to a little muscle and fat, these parts contain relatively high levels of collagen, found especially in the skin and joints. The collagen broke down into gelatin during cooking, which added thick richness to the stock. We deliberately left out breasts because they offer little collagen. Because we wanted our stock to taste as chicken-y as possible, we used only chopped onion and bay leaves for flavoring; they added just enough dimension and flavor to the stock without making it taste too vegetal. Chicken backs are often available at supermarket butcher counters during colder months. You can also save and freeze backs if you butcher whole chickens at home. For information on how to defat stock, see page 4. If you have a large pot (at least 12 quarts), you can easily double this recipe to make 1 gallon. For information on how to store and freeze stock, see page 3.

makes about 8 cups

4 pounds chicken backs and wings

14 cups water

1 onion, chopped

2 bay leaves

2 teaspoons salt

1. Heat chicken and water in large stockpot or Dutch oven over medium-high heat until boiling, skimming off any scum that comes to the surface. Reduce heat to low and simmer gently for 3 hours.

2. Add onion, bay leaves, and salt and continue to simmer for another 2 hours.

3. Strain stock through fine-mesh strainer into large pot or container, pressing on solids to extract as much liquid as possible. Let stock settle for about 5 minutes, then skim off fat.

to make ahead
Cooled stock can be refrigerated for up to 4 days or frozen for up to 1 month.

rich beef stock

why this recipe works This recipe for a rich traditional beef stock delivers a stock with great body, lots of beefy flavor, and a generous amount of meat. It took 6 pounds of beef and bones to make it. Here's why: Roasting and simmering just beef bones with some aromatic vegetables yielded beef stock that tasted like bone-enhanced vegetable liquid. We figured out that it was going to take more meat than bones to get deep beef flavor. We tested different cuts of beef and shanks, a common supermarket cut with exposed marrow bones, were our favorite, followed by marrow bone–enhanced chuck. Not only was the shank meat soft and gelatinous, it was perfect for shredding and adding to our beef soups (page 58). We used one lone onion as our vegetable and enlivened the stock with a modest ½ cup of red wine. Unlike other traditional stocks, ours was done in about 2½ hours and was a one-pot, stovetop-only affair. Note that you need only 2 cups of the cooked beef for our soups, but the leftover beef is delicious and also good for sandwiches. For more information on how to defat stock, see page 4. Use a Dutch oven or stockpot that holds 6 quarts or more for this recipe. For information on how to store and freeze stock, see page 3.

makes about 8 cups stock and 6 cups meat

2 tablespoons vegetable oil

1 large onion, chopped

6 pounds beef shanks, meat removed from bones and cut into large chunks, bones reserved, or 4 pounds beef chuck, cut into 3-inch chunks, plus 2 pounds marrow bones

½ cup dry red wine

8 cups boiling water

2 bay leaves

½ teaspoon salt

1. Heat 1 tablespoon oil in stockpot or Dutch oven over medium-high heat until shimmering. Add onion and cook, stirring occasionally, until slightly softened, 2 to 3 minutes. Transfer to large bowl.

2. Brown meat and bones on all sides in 3 or 4 batches, about 5 minutes per batch, adding remaining oil to pot as necessary; do not overcrowd. Transfer to bowl with onion. Add wine to pot and cook, scraping up any browned bits, until wine is reduced to about 3 tablespoons, about 2 minutes. Return browned beef and onion to pot. Reduce heat to low, cover, and cook until meat releases its juices, about 20 minutes. Increase heat to high; add boiling water, bay leaves, and salt. Bring to boil, then reduce heat to low, cover, and simmer slowly until meat is tender and stock is flavorful, 1½ to 2 hours, skimming foam off surface. Strain stock through fine-mesh strainer and discard bones and onion; reserve meat for soup or other use.

3. Let stock settle for 5 to 10 minutes, then defat using wide, shallow spoon or fat separator.

to make ahead
Cooled stock and meat can be refrigerated separately for up to 4 days or frozen for up to 1 month before being used to make soup.

cheater chicken broth

why this recipe works Having a quick-to-make chicken broth is essential for soups as well as numerous other uses in cooking. We wanted one that was not only full of chicken flavor but also had a good viscous consistency. To quickly improve the flavor of store-bought broth, we skipped the bones and started by browning ground chicken, which has lots of surface area and thus gives up its flavor fast. Simmering the sautéed ground meat in the broth for just 30 minutes gave the broth a significant flavor boost. Because this broth isn't made with gelatin-rich bones or skin, we devised a quick fix: unflavored powdered gelatin. Adding 1 teaspoon per cup of liquid gave our broth surprisingly good body. For the best flavor, we kept it simple and added only onion and bay leaves. Since store-bought broth contains almost no fat, leave a little on the broth's surface when skimming to enhance its flavor. Both dark and white meat ground chicken will work in this recipe. Our favorite store-bought chicken broth is Swanson Chicken Stock (see page 3). For information on how to defat broth, see page 4. For information on how to store and freeze broth, see page 3.

makes about 8 cups

1 tablespoon vegetable oil

1 pound ground chicken

1 onion, chopped

4 cups water

4 cups chicken broth

8 teaspoons unflavored gelatin

2 bay leaves

2 teaspoons salt

1. Heat oil in large saucepan over medium-high heat until shimmering. Add chicken and onion and cook, stirring frequently, until chicken is no longer pink, 5 to 10 minutes.

2. Add water, broth, gelatin, bay leaves, and salt and bring to simmer. Reduce heat to medium-low, cover, and cook for 30 minutes. Strain broth through fine-mesh strainer into large pot or container, pressing on solids to extract as much liquid as possible. Let broth settle for about 5 minutes, then skim off fat.

to make ahead
Cooled broth can be refrigerated for up to 4 days or frozen for up to 1 month.

cheater beef broth

why this recipe works This simple beef broth is a great homemade stand-in when there isn't time to make our classic Rich Beef Stock (page 168); it is a wonderful base for soups as well as gravies and pan sauces. Since store-bought beef broth contains almost no beef, we found we could doctor it to amp up its flavor—by adding real beef. We chose ground beef because it releases its flavor fairly quickly; plus it's convenient and relatively inexpensive. Browning the beef created a flavorful fond on the bottom of the pan while gently simmering the bits of beef in the broth released more flavor. Because we weren't using collagen-rich bones, we needed to use powdered gelatin to give our broth body. Adding 1 teaspoon of gelatin per cup of liquid did the trick. We prefer the flavor of 85 percent lean ground beef, but 90 percent lean beef can be used. Our favorite store-bought beef broth is Better Than Bouillon Beef Base (see page 3). For information on how to defat broth, see page 4. For information on how to store and freeze broth, see page 3.

makes about 8 cups

1 teaspoon vegetable oil

1 pound 85 percent ground beef

8 cups beef broth

8 teaspoons unflavored gelatin

1. Heat oil in large saucepan over medium-high heat until shimmering. Add beef to pot, breaking into rough 1-inch chunks. Cook, stirring occasionally, until beef is browned and fond develops on pan bottom, 6 to 8 minutes.

2. Add broth and gelatin and bring to simmer, scraping up any browned bits. Reduce heat to medium-low and gently simmer, covered, for 30 minutes. Strain broth through fine-mesh strainer into large pot or container, pressing on solids to extract as much liquid as possible. Let broth settle for about 5 minutes, then skim off fat.

to make ahead
Cooled broth can be refrigerated for up to 4 days or frozen for up to 1 month.

beef bone broth

why this recipe works Our deeply flavorful, nuanced beef broth can be used in recipes or enjoyed as a drinking broth. We started with the most important ingredient: the beef. Many recipes call for roasting beef bones, but these broths didn't have much beefy flavor; using meat alone produced thin broths that lacked body. Finally, we settled on oxtails—they were economical, widely available, and served as all-in-one bundles of flavor-packed meat, fat, collagen-rich connective tissue, and bone marrow. Plus, since they're sold precut, the oxtails didn't require any special preparation. To extract the most flavor, we browned them first to create fond and then simmered the broth for 24 hours: This broth had a beautiful mahogany color, rich beefy flavor, and luxurious, silky texture. An onion, a bit of tomato paste, and bay leaves enhanced the broth's meaty flavor while adding a touch of aromatic sweetness, and white mushrooms played a crucial role in rounding out the overall flavor with their savory tones. We found that the long, slow simmer could be accomplished in a 200-degree oven or in a slow cooker set on low, keeping our recipe streamlined and hands-off. Try to buy oxtails that are approximately 2 inches thick and 2 to 4 inches in diameter; they will yield more flavor for the broth. Oxtails can often be found in the freezer section of the grocery store; if using frozen oxtails, be sure to thaw them completely before using. For more information on how to defat broth, see page 4. If using a slow cooker, you will need one that holds 5½ to 7 quarts. For information on how to store and freeze broth, see page 3.

2 tablespoons extra-virgin olive oil

6 pounds oxtails

1 large onion, chopped

8 ounces white mushrooms, trimmed and chopped

2 tablespoons tomato paste

10 cups water

3 bay leaves

Kosher salt and pepper

1. Heat 1 tablespoon oil in Dutch oven over medium-high heat until just smoking. Pat oxtails dry with paper towels. Brown half of oxtails, 7 to 10 minutes; transfer to large bowl. Repeat with remaining 1 tablespoon oil and remaining oxtails; transfer to bowl.

2. Add onion and mushrooms to fat left in pot and cook until softened and lightly browned, about 5 minutes. Stir in tomato paste and cook until fragrant, about 1 minute. Stir in 2 cups water, bay leaves, 1 teaspoon salt, and ¼ teaspoon pepper, scraping up any browned bits.

3a. for the oven Adjust oven rack to middle position and heat oven to 200 degrees. Stir remaining 8 cups water into pot, then return browned oxtails and any accumulated juices to pot and bring to simmer. Fit large piece of aluminum foil over pot, pressing to seal, then cover tightly with lid. Transfer pot to oven and cook until broth is rich and flavorful, about 24 hours.

3b. for the slow cooker Transfer browned oxtails and any accumulated juices and vegetable mixture to slow cooker. Stir in remaining 8 cups water. Cover and cook until broth is rich and flavorful, about 24 hours on low.

4. Remove oxtails, then strain broth through fine-mesh strainer into large container; discard solids. Let broth settle for 5 to 10 minutes, then defat using wide, shallow spoon or fat separator.

to make ahead
Cooled broth can be refrigerated for up to 4 days or frozen for up to 1 month.

vegetable broth base

why this recipe works Our vegetable broth base delivers on both great flavor and convenience. The broth bases found on supermarket shelves promise an economical alternative to liquid broth, but they usually deliver harsh, overwhelming flavors. To make a vegetable concentrate that would pack bold but balanced flavor, we started with a classic *mirepoix* of onion, carrots, and celery. However, the celery gave the broth a bitter flavor, and the onion was too pungent. We swapped in celery root and leeks, which lent similar but milder flavors. Some parsley added a fresh, herbal note. To amp up the savory flavor and give the broth more depth and complexity, we added dried onion, tomato paste, and soy sauce. A hefty dose of salt ensured that the broth was well seasoned and kept the base from freezing solid, so we could store it in the freezer for months and easily remove a tablespoon at a time without having to thaw the container. For the best balance of flavors, measure the prepped vegetables by weight. Kosher salt aids in grinding the vegetables.

makes about 1¾ cups base, or about 1¾ gallons broth

2 leeks, white and light green parts only, chopped, and washed thoroughly (2½ cups, 5 ounces)

2 carrots, peeled and cut into ½-inch pieces (⅔ cup, 3 ounces)

½ small celery root, peeled and cut into ½-inch pieces (¾ cup, 3 ounces)

½ cup (½ ounce) fresh parsley leaves and thin stems

3 tablespoons dried minced onion

2 tablespoons kosher salt

1½ tablespoons tomato paste

3 tablespoons soy sauce

1. Process leeks, carrots, celery root, parsley, dried minced onion, and salt in food processor, pausing to scrape down sides of bowl frequently, until paste is as fine as possible, 3 to 4 minutes. Add tomato paste and process for 1 minute, scraping down sides of bowl every 20 seconds. Add soy sauce and continue to process for 1 minute. Transfer mixture to airtight container and tap firmly on counter to remove air bubbles. Press small piece of parchment paper flush against surface of mixture and cover tightly. Freeze for up to 6 months.

2. to make 1 cup broth Stir 1 tablespoon fresh or frozen broth base into 1 cup boiling water. If particle-free broth is desired, let broth steep for 5 minutes, then strain through fine-mesh strainer.

conversions and equivalents

converting fahrenheit to celsius
We include temperatures in some of the recipes in this book and we recommend an instant-read thermometer for the job. To convert Fahrenheit degrees to Celsius, use this simple formula:

Subtract 32 degrees from the Fahrenheit reading, then divide the result by 1.8 to find the Celsius reading. For example: "Cover and simmer gently until chicken registers 160 degrees, about 10 minutes."

To convert
$160°F - 32 = 128°$
$128° ÷ 1.8 = 71.11°C$
　　　　rounded down to 71°C

Some say cooking is a science and an art. We would say that geography has a hand in it, too. Flour milled in the United Kingdom and elsewhere will feel and taste different from flour milled in the United States. So we cannot promise that the bread you bake in Canada or England will taste the same as bread baked in the States, but we can offer guidelines for converting weights and measures. We also recommend that you rely on your instincts when making our recipes. Refer to the visual cues provided.

The recipes in this book were developed using standard U.S. measures following U.S. government guidelines. The charts below offer equivalents for U.S. and metric measures. All conversions are approximate and have been rounded up or down to the nearest whole number. For example:

1 teaspoon = 4.9292 milliliters, rounded up to 5 milliliters
1 ounce = 28.3495 grams, rounded down to 28 grams

volume conversions

U.S.	metric
1 teaspoon	5 milliliters
2 teaspoons	10 milliliters
1 tablespoon	15 milliliters
2 tablespoons	30 milliliters
¼ cup	59 milliliters
⅓ cup	79 milliliters
½ cup	118 milliliters
¾ cup	177 milliliters
1 cup	237 milliliters
1¼ cups	296 milliliters
1½ cups	355 milliliters
2 cups (1 pint)	473 milliliters
2½ cups	591 milliliters
3 cups	710 milliliters
4 cups (1 quart)	0.946 liter
1.06 quarts	1 liter
4 quarts (1 gallon)	3.8 liters

weight conversions

ounces	grams
½	14
¾	21
1	28
1½	43
2	57
2½	71
3	85
3½	99
4	113
4½	128
5	142
6	170
7	198
8	227
9	255
10	283
12	340
16 (1 pound)	454

index

Note: Page references in *italics* indicate photographs.

A

Almond and Garlic Soup,
      Spanish Chilled (White
      Gazpacho), *134,* 135
Apple
      and Butternut Squash Soup,
            Curried, 126
      Celeriac, and Fennel Chowder, 84, *85*
Artichoke Soup à la Barigoule, 100, *101*
Avocados
      Tortilla Soup, *44,* 45

B

Baby Carrot Bisque with Goat
      Cheese, *24, 25*
Bacon
      Bits, Candied, 124, *125*
      flavoring soup with, 8
Barley
      and Beef Soup, Quick, 18, *19*
      Beef Soup with Mushrooms and
            Thyme, 58, *59*
      and Vegetable Soup,
            Farmhouse, *92,* 93
Basil
      Hearty Minestrone, 140, *141*
      in Pistou, 90, *91*
Bay leaves, flavoring soup with, 8
Bean(s)
      Black, Soup, 158, *159*
      Black, Soup, Easy Vegetarian, 33
      Black, Soup with Chipotle
            Chiles, 158
      Black, Soup with Chorizo,
            Easy, *32,* 33
      15-, and Vegetable Soup,
            Hearty, *156,* 157
      Hearty Minestrone, 140, *141*
      Mexican-Style Chicken and Chickpea
            Soup, 48, *49*

Bean(s) *(cont.)*
      Moroccan-Style Chickpea
            Soup, 154, *155*
      Navy, Soup, U.S. Senate, 160, *161*
      Pasta e Fagioli, *142,* 143
      Pasta e Fagioli with Orange and
            Fennel, 143
      Provençal Vegetable Soup (Soupe au
            Pistou), 90, *91*
      Ribollita, 144
      Sicilian Chickpea and Escarole
            Soup, *152,* 153
      Spicy Moroccan-Style Lamb and
            Lentil Soup (Harira), *56,* 57
      Split Pea and Ham Soup, *162,* 163
      White, Country-Style Potato-Leek
            Soup with, 97
      White, Soup, Tuscan, 144, *145*
      see also Green beans; Lentil(s)
Beef
      and Barley Soup, Quick, 18, *19*
      Barley Soup with Mushrooms and
            Thyme, 58, *59*
      Bone Broth, *172,* 173
      Broth, Cheater, 171
      broth, taste tests on, 3
      and Cabbage Soup, Russian-
            Style, 64, *65*
      Italian Wedding Soup, 62, 63
      Noodle Soup with Mushrooms and
            Thyme, 58
      Pho, Vietnamese, *66,* 67
      and Ramen Soup, 17
      Stock, Rich, 168, *169*
      and Vegetable Soup, Mexican, 60, *61*
      and Vegetable Soup, Quick, *20,* 21
Beet(s)
      Chilled Borscht, 136, *137*
      and Wheat Berry Soup with Dill
            Cream, 102, *103*
Best Mushroom Bisque, *118,* 119
Black Bean Soup, 158, *159*

Black Bean Soup with Chipotle
      Chiles, 158
Blender, 6
Bok choy
      Vegetable Shabu-Shabu with Sesame
            Sauce, *104,* 105
Borscht
      Chilled, 136, *137*
      garnishes for, 136
Breads
      Cheese Croutons, for Ultimate
            French Onion Soup, 106, *107*
      Classic Croutons; var., 11, *11*
      Easy Dinner Rolls, 10
      Easy Garlic Rolls, 10
      Garlic Toasts, 11
      Rosemary-Olive Focaccia, 10, *10*
      Soft and Cheesy Breadsticks, 10
Broccoli-Cheese Soup, *128,* 129
Broth
      Base, Vegetable, 174, *175*
      Beef, Cheater, 171
      Beef Bone, *172,* 173
      Chicken, Cheater, 170
      freezing, 3
      store-bought, taste tests on, 3
Bulgur, Tomato, and Red Pepper
      Soup, Turkish, 26, *27*
Buttery Rye Croutons, 11

C

Cabbage
      Beef and Ramen Soup, 17
      and Beef Soup, Russian-Style, 64, *65*
      Beet and Wheat Berry Soup with Dill
            Cream, 102, *103*
      Chicken and Ramen Soup, *16,* 17
      Farmhouse Vegetable and Barley
            Soup, *92,* 93
      Hearty Minestrone, 140, *141*
      Soup, Hearty, *98,* 99

Caldo Verde, 22, *23*
Candied Bacon Bits, 124, *125*
Carrot
  Baby, Bisque with Goat
    Cheese, *24,* 25
  -Ginger Soup, Great, *114,* 115
Cauliflower
  Soup, Creamy, 116, *117*
  Soup, Curried, 116
Celeriac, Fennel, and Apple
    Chowder, 84, *85*
Chard
  Hearty 15-Bean and Vegetable
    Soup, *156,* 157
  Italian Wedding Soup, *62,* 63
  Super Greens Soup with Lemon-
    Tarragon Cream, 88, *89*
Cheater Beef Broth, 171
Cheater Chicken Broth, 170
Cheese
  -Broccoli Soup, *128,* 129
  Croutons, for Ultimate French Onion
    Soup, 106, *107*
  crumbled, garnishing with, 9
  Goat, Baby Carrot Bisque with, *24, 25*
  Italian Chicken Soup with Parmesan
    Dumplings, *50,* 51
  Italian Wedding Soup, *62, 63*
  Parmesan, flavoring soup with, 8
  Pistou, 90, *91*
  Soft and Cheesy Breadsticks, 10
  Tortilla Soup, *44,* 45
Chef's knife, 7
Chicken
  Broth, Cheater, 170
  broth, taste tests on, 3
  and Chickpea Soup, Mexican-
    Style, 48, *49*
  Chowder, Farmhouse, 73
  Chowder, Farmhouse, with
    Corn, Poblano Chile, and
    Cilantro, *72,* 73
  Matzo Ball Soup, 42, *43*
  Mulligatawny with, *54,* 55
  Noodle Soup, Classic, *40,* 41

Chicken *(cont.)*
  Noodle Soup, Weeknight, 15
  and Ramen Soup, *16,* 17
  and Rice Soup, Weeknight, *14,* 15
  Soup, Hearty Cream of, 46, *47*
  Soup, Italian, Parmesan
    Dumplings, *50,* 51
  Soup, Thai-Style, 52, *53*
  Stock, Classic, *166,* 167
  Tortilla Soup, *44,* 45
Chicken fat, skimming and storing, 8
Chile(s)
  Chipotle, and Lime, Spicy Gazpacho
    with, 110
  Chipotle, Black Bean Soup with, 158
  Poblano, Corn, and Cilantro,
    Farmhouse Chicken Chowder
    with, *72,* 73
  Southwestern Butternut Squash
    Soup, 126
  Spicy Thai-Style Shrimp Soup, *28, 29*
  Thai-Style Chicken Soup, 52, *53*
  White Lentil Soup with Coconut Milk
    and Mustard Greens, 150, *151*
Chilled Borscht, 136, *137*
Chowders, list of, 71
Cilantro
  Easy Black Bean Soup with
    Chorizo, *32, 33*
  Easy Vegetarian Black Bean Soup, 33
  Vietnamese Beef Pho, *66,* 67
Cilantro Cream and Smoked Paprika,
    Roasted Red Pepper Soup
    with, 120, *121*
Cinnamon-Sugar Croutons, 11
Citrus
  garnishing with, 9
  zest, freezing, 6
Clam
  Chowder, Italian-Style Manhattan, 77
  Chowder, Manhattan, *76,* 77
  Chowder, New England, 74, *75*
  juice, taste tests on, 3
Classic Chicken Noodle Soup, *40,* 41

Classic Chicken Stock, *166,* 167
Classic Croutons; var., 11, *11*
Classic Gazpacho, 110, *111*
Coconut Milk
  and Mustard Greens, White Lentil
    Soup with, 150, *151*
  Thai-Style Chicken Soup, 52, *53*
Cod
  New England Fish Chowder, 78, *79*
  Provençal Fish Soup, 38, *39*
Corn
  Chowder, Fresh, *82,* 83
  and Lobster Chowder, *80,* 81
  Mexican Beef and Vegetable
    Soup, 60, *61*
  Poblano Chile, and Cilantro,
    Farmhouse Chicken Chowder
    with, *72,* 73
Country-Style Potato-Leek Soup, 97
Country-Style Potato-Leek Soup with
    Kielbasa, *96,* 97
Country-Style Potato-Leek Soup with
    White Beans, 97
Creamless Creamy Tomato
    Soup, *122,* 123
Creamy Butternut Squash
    Soup, 126, *127*
Creamy Butternut Squash Soup with
    Fennel, 126
Creamy Cauliflower Soup, 116, *117*
Croutons
  Cheese, for Ultimate French Onion
    Soup, 106, *107*
  Classic; var., 11, *11*
Cucumbers
  Classic Gazpacho, 110, *111*
  Spicy Gazpacho with Chipotle Chile
    and Lime, 110
Curried Butternut Squash and Apple
    Soup, 126
Curried Cauliflower Soup, 116
Curried Lentil Soup with Spinach, 149
Curried Red Lentil Soup, 30, *31*
Curried Vegetarian Lentil
    Soup, *148,* 149

D

Dairy, freezing soups with, 5
Dill Cream, Beet and Wheat Berry
  Soup with, 102, *103*
Dumplings, Parmesan, Italian
  Chicken Soup with, *50,* 51
Dutch oven, 6

E

Easy Black Bean Soup with
  Chorizo, *32,* 33
Easy Dinner Rolls, 10
Easy Garlic Rolls, 10
Easy Vegetarian Black Bean Soup, 33
11th-Hour Harvest Pumpkin Soup,
  34, *35*
Equipment, 6–7
Escarole
  and Chickpea Soup, Sicilian, *152,* 153
  Italian Chicken Soup with Parmesan
    Dumplings, *50,* 51

F

Farmhouse Chicken Chowder, 73
Farmhouse Chicken Chowder with
  Corn, Poblano Chile, and
  Cilantro, *72,* 73
Farmhouse Vegetable and Barley
  Soup, *92,* 93
Fat separator, 7
Fennel
  Celeriac, and Apple Chowder, 84, *85*
  Creamy Butternut Squash Soup
    with, 126
  Italian Chicken Soup with Parmesan
    Dumplings, *50,* 51
  and Orange, Pasta e Fagioli with, 143
  Provençal Fish Soup, 38, *39*
  Sicilian Chickpea and Escarole
    Soup, *152,* 153
Fine-mesh strainer, 6

Fish

Chowder, New England, 78, *79*
Soup, Provençal, 38, *39*
Focaccia, Rosemary-Olive, 10, *10*
Fresh Corn Chowder, *82,* 83

G

Garlic
  and Almond Soup, Spanish Chilled
    (White Gazpacho), *134,* 135
  Chips, *108,* 109
  Croutons, 11
  minced, freezing, 6
  -Potato Soup, *108,* 109
  Rolls, Easy, 10
  Toasts, 11
Garnishes, 9–11
Gazpacho
  Classic, 110, *111*
  Spicy, with Chipotle Chile and
    Lime, 110
  White (Spanish Chilled Almond and
    Garlic Soup), *134,* 135
Ginger
  -Carrot Soup, Great, *114,* 115
  Curried Red Lentil Soup, 30, *31*
  grated, freezing, 6
  Mulligatawny with Chicken, *54,* 55
  Vietnamese Beef Pho, *66,* 67
Grains
  Beef Barley Soup with Mushrooms
    and Thyme, 58, *59*
  Beet and Wheat Berry Soup with Dill
    Cream, 102, *103*
  Farmhouse Vegetable and Barley
    Soup, *92,* 93
  Quick Beef and Barley Soup, 18, *19*
  Turkish Tomato, Bulgur, and Red
    Pepper Soup, 26, *27*
  Weeknight Chicken and Rice
    Soup, *14,* 15
  Wild Rice and Mushroom
    Soup, 94, *95*

Grapes

Spanish Chilled Almond and Garlic
  Soup (White Gazpacho), *134,* 135
Great Carrot-Ginger Soup, *114,* 115
Green beans
  Provençal Vegetable Soup (Soupe au
    Pistou), 90, *91*
  Quick Beef and Vegetable Soup, *20,* 21
Greens
  Caldo Verde, 22, *23*
  Hearty 15-Bean and Vegetable
    Soup, *156,* 157
  Hearty Spanish-Style Lentil and
    Chorizo Soup with Kale, 146, *147*
  Italian Chicken Soup with Parmesan
    Dumplings, *50,* 51
  Italian Wedding Soup, *62,* 63
  Mustard, and Coconut Milk, White
    Lentil Soup with, 150, *151*
  Sicilian Chickpea and Escarole
    Soup, *152,* 153
  Super, Soup with Lemon-Tarragon
    Cream, 88, *89*
  see also Cabbage; Spinach

H

Ham
  Black Bean Soup, 158, *159*
  Black Bean Soup with Chipotle
    Chiles, 158
  and Split Pea Soup, *162,* 163
  U.S. Senate Navy Bean Soup, 160, *161*
Harira (Spicy Moroccan-Style Lamb
  and Lentil Soup), *56,* 57
Hearty 15-Bean and Vegetable
  Soup, *156,* 157
Hearty Cabbage Soup, *98,* 99
Hearty Cream of Chicken Soup, 46, *47*
Hearty Minestrone, 140, *141*
Hearty Spanish-Style Lentil and
  Chorizo Soup, 146
Hearty Spanish-Style Lentil and
  Chorizo Soup with Kale, 146, *147*

Herbed Croutons, 11
Herbs
    Dill Cream, 102
    fresh, flavoring soup with, 8
    Hearty Minestrone, 140, *141*
    Pistou, 90, *91*
    Rosemary-Olive Focaccia, 10, *10*
    Super Greens Soup with Lemon-
        Tarragon Cream, 88, *89*
    see also Cilantro

I

Italian Chicken Soup with Parmesan
    Dumplings, *50,* 51
Italian-Style Manhattan Clam
    Chowder, 77
Italian Wedding Soup, *62,* 63

K

Kale
    Hearty Spanish-Style Lentil and
        Chorizo Soup with, 146, *147*
    Italian Wedding Soup, *62,* 63
    Super Greens Soup with Lemon-
        Tarragon Cream, 88, *89*
Knives, 7

L

Ladle, 6
Lamb and Lentil Soup, Spicy
    Moroccan-Style (Harira), *56, 57*
Leek-Potato Soup, Country-Style, 97
    with Kielbasa, *96,* 97
    with White Beans, 97
Lemon-Tarragon Cream, Super
    Greens Soup with, 88, *89*
Lentil(s)
    and Chorizo Soup, Hearty Spanish-
        Style, 146
    and Chorizo Soup, Hearty Spanish-
        Style, with Kale, 146, *147*

Lentil(s) *(cont.)*
    and Lamb Soup, Spicy Moroccan-
        Style (Harira), *56,* 57
    Mulligatawny with Chicken, *54,* 55
    Red, Soup, Curried, 30, *31*
    Soup, Curried, with Spinach, 149
    Soup, Curried Vegetarian, *148,* 149
    White, Soup with Coconut Milk and
        Mustard Greens, 150, *151*
Lime and Chipotle Chile, Spicy
    Gazpacho with, 110
Lobster
    Bisque, 132, *133*
    and Corn Chowder, *80,* 81
    Seafood Bisque, 131

M

Manhattan Clam Chowder, *76, 77*
Maple Sour Cream, 124
Matzo Ball Soup, 42, *43*
Meat. *See* Beef; Lamb; Pork
Meat cleaver, 7
Mexican Beef and Vegetable
    Soup, 60, *61*
Mexican-Style Chicken and Chickpea
    Soup, 48, *49*
Minestrone, Hearty, 140, *141*
Moroccan-Style Chickpea Soup, 154, *155*
Mulligatawny with Chicken, *54,* 55
Mushroom(s)
    Artichoke Soup à la Barigoule, 100, *101*
    Bisque, Best, *118,* 119
    Hearty 15-Bean and Vegetable
        Soup, *156,* 157
    Spicy Thai-Style Shrimp Soup, *28,* 29
    Thai-Style Chicken Soup, 52, *53*
    and Thyme, Beef Barley Soup with,
        58, *59*
    and Thyme, Beef Noodle Soup with, 58
    Vegetable Shabu-Shabu with Sesame
        Sauce, *104,* 105
    and Wild Rice Soup, 94, *95*
Mustard Greens and Coconut Milk,
    White Lentil Soup with, 150, *151*

N

New England Clam Chowder, 74, *75*
New England Fish Chowder, 78, *79*
Noodle(s)
    Beef and Ramen Soup, 17
    Chicken and Ramen Soup, *16,* 17
    Ramen Soup with Pork, *68,* 69
    Soup, Beef, with Mushrooms and
        Thyme, 58
    Soup, Classic Chicken, *40,* 41
    Soup, Weeknight Chicken, 15
    Vegetable Shabu-Shabu with Sesame
        Sauce, *104,* 105
    Vietnamese Beef Pho, *66,* 67
Nuts
    Spanish Chilled Almond and Garlic
        Soup (White Gazpacho), *134,* 135
    toasted, garnishing with, 9

O

Olive oil, garnishing with, 9
Olive-Rosemary Focaccia, 10, *10*
Onion Soup, Ultimate French, 106, *107*
Orange and Fennel, Pasta e Fagioli
    with, 143

P

Parsnips
    Artichoke Soup à la Barigoule, 100, *101*
    Matzo Ball Soup, 42, *43*
Pasta
    e Fagioli, *142,* 143
    e Fagioli with Orange and Fennel, 143
    freezing soups with, 5
    Italian Wedding Soup, *62,* 63
    Provençal Vegetable Soup (Soupe au
        Pistou), 90, *91*
Pea, Split, and Ham Soup, *162,* 163
Pepper(s)
    Classic Gazpacho, 110, *111*
    Farmhouse Chicken Chowder, 73
    Red, Tomato, and Bulgur Soup,
        Turkish, 26, *27*

Pepper(s) *(cont.)*

Roasted Red, Soup with Smoked Paprika and Cilantro Cream, 120, *121*

Spicy Gazpacho with Chipotle Chile and Lime, 110

see also Chile(s)

Pho, Vietnamese Beef, *66,* 67

Pistou, 90, *91*

Pork

Italian Wedding Soup, *62,* 63

Ramen Soup with, *68,* 69

see also Bacon; Ham; Sausages

Potato(es)

Caldo Verde, 22, *23*

Celeriac, Fennel, and Apple Chowder, 84, *85*

Farmhouse Chicken Chowder, 73

Farmhouse Chicken Chowder with Corn, Poblano Chile, and Cilantro, *72,* 73

Farmhouse Vegetable and Barley Soup, *92,* 93

Fresh Corn Chowder, *82,* 83

-Garlic Soup, *108,* 109

Hearty Cabbage Soup, *98,* 99

Hearty Cream of Chicken Soup, 46, *47*

Italian-Style Manhattan Clam Chowder, 77

-Leek Soup, Country-Style, 97

-Leek Soup, Country-Style, with Kielbasa, *96,* 97

-Leek Soup, Country-Style, with White Beans, 97

Manhattan Clam Chowder, *76,* 77

Mexican Beef and Vegetable Soup, 60, *61*

Moroccan-Style Chickpea Soup, 154, *155*

New England Clam Chowder, 74, *75*

New England Fish Chowder, 78, *79*

Quick Beef and Vegetable Soup, *20,* 21

Sweet, Soup, 124, *125*

U.S. Senate Navy Bean Soup, 160, *161*

Provençal Fish Soup, 38, *39*

Provençal Vegetable Soup (Soupe au Pistou), 90, *91*

Pumpkin Soup, 11th-Hour Harvest, 34, *35*

Q

Quick Beef and Barley Soup, 18, *19*

Quick Beef and Vegetable Soup, *20,* 21

R

Ramen Soup with Pork, *68,* 69

Ribollita, 144

Rice

and Chicken Soup, Weeknight, *14,* 15

Wild, and Mushroom Soup, *94,* 95

Rich Beef Stock, 168, *169*

Roasted Red Pepper Soup with Smoked Paprika and Cilantro Cream, 120, *121*

Rosemary-Olive Focaccia, 10, *10*

Russian-Style Beef and Cabbage Soup, 64, *65*

S

Sausages

Caldo Verde, 22, *23*

Country-Style Potato-Leek Soup with Kielbasa, *96,* 97

Easy Black Bean Soup with Chorizo, *32,* 33

Hearty Spanish-Style Lentil and Chorizo Soup, 146

Hearty Spanish-Style Lentil and Chorizo Soup with Kale, 146, *147*

Seafood

Bisque, 131

Italian-Style Manhattan Clam Chowder, 77

Lobster and Corn Chowder, *80,* 81

Lobster Bisque, 132, *133*

Manhattan Clam Chowder, *76,* 77

New England Clam Chowder, 74, *75*

Seafood *(cont.)*

New England Fish Chowder, 78, *79*

Provençal Fish Soup, 38, *39*

Shrimp Bisque, *130,* 131

Spicy Thai-Style Shrimp Soup, *28,* 29

Seasoning soups, 2

Seaweed

Vegetable Shabu-Shabu with Sesame Sauce, *104,* 105

Seeds

toasted, garnishing with, 9

Vegetable Shabu-Shabu with Sesame Sauce, *104,* 105

Shabu-Shabu, Vegetable, with Sesame Sauce, *104,* 105

Shrimp

Bisque, *130,* 131

Seafood Bisque, 131

Soup, Spicy Thai-Style, *28,* 29

Sicilian Chickpea and Escarole Soup, *152,* 153

Simmering, versus boiling, 2

Smoked Paprika

and Cilantro Cream, Roasted Red Pepper Soup with, 120, *121*

Hearty Spanish-Style Lentil and Chorizo Soup, 146

Hearty Spanish-Style Lentil and Chorizo Soup with Kale, 146, *147*

Soft and Cheesy Breadsticks, 10

Soups

adding flavor to, 8

all-time best tips, 2

cooling, 5

defatting, 4

equipment for, 6–7

freezing single servings, 5

garnish ideas, 9

pureeing, 4

reheating, 5

serving, 9

store-bought broths for, 3

storing, 5

thawing, 5

too thick or thin, rescuing, 8

Sour Cream
Cilantro Cream, 120, *121*
Dill Cream, 102
garnishing with, 9
Maple, 124
Southwestern Butternut Squash Soup, 126
Spanish Chilled Almond and Garlic Soup (White Gazpacho), *134,* 135
Spicy Gazpacho with Chipotle Chile and Lime, 110
Spicy Moroccan-Style Lamb and Lentil Soup (Harira), *56,* 57
Spicy Thai-Style Shrimp Soup, *28,* 29
Spinach
Beef and Ramen Soup, 17
Broccoli-Cheese Soup, *128,* 129
Chicken and Ramen Soup, *16,* 17
Curried Lentil Soup with, 149
Split Pea and Ham Soup, *162,* 163
Spoons, 6
Squash
Butternut, and Apple Soup, Curried, 126
Butternut, Soup, Creamy, 126, *127*
Butternut, Soup, Creamy, with Fennel, 126
Butternut, Soup, Southwestern, 126
11th-Hour Harvest Pumpkin Soup, 34, *35*
see also Zucchini
Stock
Beef, Rich, 168, *169*
Chicken, Classic, *166,* 167
flavorful, importance of, 2
Stockpot, 7
Super Greens Soup with Lemon-Tarragon Cream, 88, *89*
Sweet Potato Soup, 124, *125*

T

Tarragon-Lemon Cream, Super Greens Soup with, 88, *89*
Thai-Style Chicken Soup, 52, *53*
Tofu
Vegetable Shabu-Shabu with Sesame Sauce, *104,* 105
Tomato(es)
Bulgur, and Red Pepper Soup, Turkish, 26, *27*
Classic Gazpacho, 110, *111*
Italian-Style Manhattan Clam Chowder, 77
Manhattan Clam Chowder, *76,* 77
Moroccan-Style Chickpea Soup, 154, *155*
Pasta e Fagioli, *142,* 143
Pasta e Fagioli with Orange and Fennel, 143
Soup, Creamless Creamy, *122,* 123
Spicy Gazpacho with Chipotle Chile and Lime, 110
Tortilla Soup, *44,* 45
Turkish Tomato, Bulgur, and Red Pepper Soup, 26, *27*
Tuscan White Bean Soup, 144, *145*

U

Ultimate French Onion Soup, 106, *107*
U.S. Senate Navy Bean Soup, 160, *161*

V

Vegetable(s)
and 15-Bean Soup, Hearty, *156,* 157
aromatic, sautéing, 2
and Barley Soup, Farmhouse, *92,* 93
and Beef Soup, Mexican, 60, *61*
and Beef Soup, Quick, *20,* 21

Vegetable(s) *(cont.)*
broth, taste tests on, 3
Broth Base, 174, *175*
cutting to right size, 2
garnishing with, 9
Shabu-Shabu with Sesame Sauce, *104,* 105
Soup, Provençal (Soupe au Pistou), 90, *91*
staggering addition of, 2
see also specific vegetables
Vietnamese Beef Pho, *66,* 67

W

Weeknight Chicken and Rice Soup, *14,* 15
Weeknight Chicken Noodle Soup, 15
Wheat Berry and Beet Soup with Dill Cream, 102, *103*
Whisk, 7
Wild Rice and Mushroom Soup, 94, *95*

Y

Yogurt, garnishing with, 9

Z

Zucchini
Hearty Minestrone, 140, *141*
Mexican Beef and Vegetable Soup, 60, *61*
Mexican-Style Chicken and Chickpea Soup, 48, *49*
Moroccan-Style Chickpea Soup, 154, *155*
Provençal Vegetable Soup (Soupe au Pistou), 90, *91*